INFLATION

Other Platform Books

Tragedy and Social Evolution: Eva Figes
Community politics Ed. Peter Hain
No Shining Armour: Edward Milne
New Enlightenment: N.A. Smith
Innovation: William Kingston
Music, Society, Education: Christopher Small
The Anti-Oedipus: Gilles Deleuze and Felix Guattari
Poulson: A Portrait of the Architect as a Young Man Michael Gillard and Martin Tomkinson

A PLATFORM BOOK

INFLATION

Michael Jefferson · Andrew Dickson White
Thomas Mann · Walt Rostow

With a foreword by John Pardoe M.P.

John Calder
LONDON

First published in Great Britain 1977
by John Calder (Publishers) Ltd
18 Brewer Street, London W1R 4AS

The Witches Sabbath by Thomas Mann published in *Encounter* February 1975
Inflation: How We Can Cure It by Walt Rostow published in *The Listener* 17th July 1975

ISBN 0 7145 3539 7 casebound
0 7145 3547 8 paperback

Photoset in 11pt Times by Specialised Offset Services Ltd, Liverpool
and printed in Great Britain by M. & A. Thomson Litho Ltd., East Kilbride, Scotland

CONTENTS

Sources of Charts

1-2 *U.K. Prices of a Composite Unit of Consumables, AD. 1260-1976*, E.H. Phelps Brown and Sheila V. Hopkins: 'Seven Centuries of the Prices of Consumables, Compared with Builders' Wage Rates', Economica, November 1956. Appendix B. Updated by the author.

3 *U.K. Prices, 1660-1910*, Elizabeth B. Schumpeter: 'English Prices and Public Finance, 1660-1822', Review of Economic Statistics, 1938. For period 1661-1697, and linked by author for 1696-1832. The period 1832-1910 is based on P. Rousseaux: 'Les Mouvements de Fond de l'Economie Anglaise, 1800-1913', 1938 (Brussels). Linked by the author, this index has a different basis from the Schumpeter-Gilboy index above and should be viewed accordingly.

4 *U.K. Board of Trade Wholesale Prices, 1871-1948*, Abstract of Labour Statistics, Board of Trade Journal.

5 *U.K. Retail Prices, 1900-1963*, London and Cambridge Economic Service: 'The British Economy: Key Statistics, 1900-1970', 1971.

6 *Wholesale Prices in France and Germany: 1800-mid 1940s and in Spain 1812 to mid-1940s*, B.R. Mitchell: 'European Historical Statistics 1750-1970', 1975.

7 *Wholesale Prices in Belgium, Italy and Sweden: 1860 to mid 1940s*, B.R. Mitchell: 'European Historical Statistics, 1750-1970', 1975.

8 *Wholesale Prices in The Netherlands and Norway: 1900 to mid-1940s, and in Austria from 1922 to 1948*, B.R. Mitchell: 'European Historical Statistics, 1750-1970', 1975.

9 *Cost of Living in Belgium, France and Germany: 1840 to 1900*, B.R. Mitchell: 'European Historical Statistics, 1750-1970', 1975.

10 *Cost of Living in Italy, The Netherlands and Sweden: 1900 to 1950*, B.R. Mitchell: 'European Historical Statstics, 1750-1970', 1975.

11 *United States: Wholesale Prices, 1749-1957*, U.S. Department of Commerce (Bureau of the Census): 'Historical Statistics of the United States: Colonial Times to 1957', 1960.

12 *United States: Cost of Living, 1820-1957*, As for Chart 11.

13 *Price Indices of Private Consumption Changes, 1950-75* (a) *USA* (b) *UK* (c) *Japan* (d) *Italy* (e) *France* (f) *West Germany* (g) *The Netherlands* (h) *Iceland* O.E.C.D. and other official sources.

INTRODUCTION

Inflation has been, other than the avoidance of war and famine, probably the biggest social problem of the post-war period in most parts of the world. In creating a new political series *Platform Books*, we decided that a many-faceted book on Inflation was needed, approaching the subject both historically and from different contemporary view points. We have brought together a combination of commissioned and reprinted work that is comprehensive and thought provoking.

Andrew Dickson White's brilliant *Fiat Money* is a little known classic, an analysis of the great inflation that preceded and accompanied the French Revolution and post-revolutionary period. It is reprinted here, together with Henry Hazlitt's important introduction, by permission of the Foundation for Economic Education Inc. of Irvington-on-Hudson, New York. Thomas Mann's *The Witches' Sabbath* is a personal account of the German Inflation that started in 1913, reached its peak in the early twenties and finally collapsed late in 1923. It was first given as a lecture in the U.S.A. in 1942 and published in the February 1976 edition of *Encounter*, with whose kind permission we reprint it. Walt Rostow, now Professor of Economics at the University of Texas, has studied the English economy from 1661, the time of the Restoration of the Monarchy after the Cromwellian Commonwealth, until recent times, proving that prices in 1913 were at the same level as when Charles II returned to the throne, but that a staggering escalation has taken place since. He draws some interesting conclusions, which any British Government might well heed. First given as a broadcast, it was reprinted in the *Listener* of 17th July 1975.

Michael Jefferson is currently senior professional economist with the Royal Dutch Shell Group, where he is responsible for assessing both the short and long term prospects for the world economy. His *Record of Inflation* is both a history and an analysis of past and present Inflations. In addition, he has written a tailpiece to bring together the many strands in this volume. John Pardoe, who, as economic spokesman for the British Liberal Party, is enabled to take not only an informed but a more objective view than most professional politicians, has contributed a foreword where he knocks down firmly some suggested solutions to the present crisis while indicating in what direction the solution may eventually be found.

The record of the past shows clearly enough that every Inflation has its solution, and that if the answer is not found in intelligent measures requiring the co-operation and discipline of all sections of society, it will be found in revolution, dictatorship or the misery of depression. As Thomas Mann puts it: 'Inflation is a tragedy that makes a whole people cynical, hardhearted and indifferent.' The signs are already recognizable in contemporary Britain, where for too long economic policy has smacked more of fundamentalist theology than of any willingness to look clearly at the realities of modern life and to implement even minimal policies to contain prices. By the time this book appears the choices will be even more limited, while further dithering may well have destroyed our chances of a civilized future. We hope it will contribute to new thinking and action that will avert that catastrophe.

THE PUBLISHERS

FOREWORD

The history of inflation ought to teach us that inflation has been caused by many different things at many different times. Sometimes it has been the debasement of the coinage, sometimes the excessive coining of money, sometimes over-production or the importation of too much precious metal, and all too often war.

Unfortunately there are still some people who pretend to themselves that all inflations in the past and all inflations in the future have been, or will be, caused by the same thing: the money supply.

It is a very attractive proposition with the great advantage of simplicity. If all Governments need to do to maintain stable prices is to ensure that the money supply never rises by more than the long term growth rate in the capacity of the economy to produce, they can forget about a great deal that makes modern government so confoundedly difficult. It is an argument that appeals, through some pretty tortuous logic, to both Left and Right of the political spectrum. The Right favours it because it does away with the need for Government intervention. There is clearly no need for Government to 'manage' the economy, if all it needs to do is to control the money supply. The Left, which is usually only too keen to welcome intervention, has one curious blind spot: wage bargaining. Wage bargaining must be kept free of Government intervention at all costs. Since the monetarist theory states that such intervention is useless and quite unnecessary, it is espoused by the Left.

The monetarist solution would certainly stop inflation. Of that there can be no doubt. The simplest definition of inflation is 'too much money chasing too few goods'. If the supply of money is frozen and the supply of goods does not change, the underlying general level of prices cannot rise. That does not of course mean that the prices of some goods will not rise. But if some prices rise others will have to fall and the index of all prices will remain the same.

This might work reasonably well in a self-sufficient economy. But the British economy is far from self-sufficient. We are heavily dependent on imported food and raw materials. And it is here that the monetarist solution runs up against the real world.

Let us look at what the monetarists say should have happened when OPEC increased oil prices in the autumn of 1973. Since this was not accompanied by any increase in the productive capacity of the economy, the money supply should not have been increased. People would then have cut their purchases of oil by enough to compensate for the oil price increase. To do this, however, huge sectors of British industry, which use oil, would have had to close down. Alternatively it would have been possible for people to cut their purchases of other goods to compensate for the rise in oil prices. But, quite apart from the fact that many of these other goods are imported or derive from imports and were rising in prices at that time almost as fast as oil, this would have forced other sectors of British industry to close down. So unemployment would have risen. Of course to a certain extent people had to adopt a bit of both these courses of action. They *did* cut their purchases of oil and they *did* cut down on other things as well: but by nothing like enough to compensate for the increased price of oil. The money supply was expanded to enable them to bridge the gap.

The monetarists say that this was very unfortunate and that it only put off the evil day. Perhaps so, but the alternative would have caused unemployment to rise to a level which no democratic Government could have sustained.

This illustrates neatly the fallacy which lies at the heart of the monetarist theory. It is based on a simple quantity equation: Money Supply x Velocity of Circulation = Output x Prices. Assuming that the velocity of circulation remains constant the monetarists then argue that any change in the money supply will affect only prices on the other side of the equation. But what about output? It would be perfectly possible for output to fall and prices to rise. Over the long term this would be unlikely. But in a democracy the trouble with the long term is not so much that, as Keynes said, in it we are all dead, but that in it there will be a change of Government or revolution!

The only rational approach to the increase in oil prices in 1973 was one which recognised that there had been a real transfer of

National Income from Britain to the OPEC countries, that consequently there was less income to go round, and to ration out that income among the British people so that everyone still remained in employment but at a lower standard of living. Such rationing of available income has to be done by an incomes policy. The only alternative is to allow some people to maintain their real incomes while others have none at all – i.e. are unemployed.

It is not, however, only in the aftermath of dramatic increases in the price of imported raw materials that inflation has occurred. There has been a steady rise in the rate of price increases in all the Western countries for a number of years. The monetarists claim that this has been due to an excessive increase in the money supply causing an excess demand. It is, they say, a simple case of 'demand-pull' inflation.

There is little evidence that Britain, in particular, has suffered from excess demand since the war. Certainly Governments have not lacked ample means to cut down demand where necessary, and indeed many economists have argued that their over anxious willingness to do so has caused Britain's low rate of economic growth.

It is far more likely that our post-war inflation has not been induced by excess demand but by the force of rising costs: that our inflation is 'cost-push' rather than 'demand-pull'.

As with the increase in oil prices such 'cost-push' can, and has recently, come from import prices. But for most of the post-war era import prices have not been the problem. It has been the increase in the cost of labour that has forced prices up.

Again the monetarists have their solution. If the money supply is not increased by more than the output of the economy, there will be no money to finance wage increases which exceed the increase in output. If one group of workers gets more than that it can only mean that another group of workers gets less – or becomes unemployed.

In theory, of course, this is all splendid. But the real world of practical politics is very different. Ever since Keynes showed Governments that unemployment was avoidable, Governments of all shades of political opinion have been committed to various definitions of 'full employment'. Governments cannot afford to allow one group of workers to price another group of workers out of employment. They therefore expand the money supply to meet the need.

Nor is it only the political commitment to full employment that has caused the force of 'wage-push' inflation to increase enormously in recent years. When firms and Unions were small there was a strict limit to how far an employer could allow his workforce to squeeze a wage increase out of him. *His* 'money supply' at least was limited. If he was competing against other firms he could not recoup the wage increase by charging higher prices for his goods. Only if he enjoyed a monopoly of goods, the demand for which was relatively inelastic, could he pass on the wage increase to his customers.

Today, however, firms are much larger and have a larger share of their market. Even where they compete with one another the same Union forces the same pay settlement on all of them. Since they know that all of them have had to face the same wage increase they can all make the same price increase.

The Unions too are much more likely than they were to base their arguments for more pay not on what a particular employer or even industry can afford, but on what they got out of some other employer or industry. No self-respecting Union leader can allow himself to get left behind in the rat-race. He must get for his members at least as much as some other Union leader got for his.

As the cost of labour has increased employers have sought to invest in more labour saving machinery. But the overhead costs of this are very high. It is very expensive indeed not to use it. The cost of a strike, therefore, has risen hugely. It is nearly always worthwhile to pay the men a bit more to keep working than to have them down tools.

So the commitment to full employment, the increased size of firms, the wider influence of Unions, and the capital intensive nature of modern industry, have all conspired together to increase the force of 'wage-push'.

Moreover the process is self-feeding. Most Trade Union members now expect their leaders to negotiate a higher increase than last year and regard anything less as failure. They are concerned to get real increases in purchasing power. If they expect prices to rise by 10% in the next twelve months, they will expect to get something more than that – say 12% – to cover the increase in prices and make them better off. If the net result of this year's wage increase is to put up prices next year by 12% then they will want 15% to cover it … and so on …

The only way to solve this problem is to change our method of wage determination. One way of doing this, suggested by Mr Peter Jay in his Wincott Memorial Lecture,[1] would be to offer employees so much in the way of workers' control as to change the whole balance of the game. Mr Jay's vision is of an economy made up of small self-governing worker co-operatives, each competing against the others, and thereby overcoming the monopoly element which has enabled large employers and large Trade Unions to conspire together to raise the price of labour and pass the cost on to the consumer.

There is a great deal in Mr Jay's idea but it would still require very firm Government indeed to ensure that the worker co-operatives did not simply get together to continue the present conspiracy. Government would have to outlaw nationwide wage bargaining and restrictive practices, and that would require a new political settlement to create such a Government.

The only other way to change the wage determination process is by some form of incomes policy. Most Governments since the war have tried this, but they have all been short term affairs in answer to some crisis. They are generally overtaken by their own inherent contradictions.

No Government has yet tried to work out a long term incomes policy. The difficulties are immense. No incomes policy that attempts to freeze the existing pattern of earnings has a hope of lasting for more than a year or two. But an incomes policy that allows flexibility and exceptions, whether based on productivity or sheer industrial muscle power, is bound to be shot full of holes.

In the long run an incomes policy, whether run by the Government or the Trade Unions, cannot work without some objective, generally agreed, and accepted criteria about the proper division of the National Income between wages and profits, and about differentials between different groups of employees. That requires a national consensus about the sort of economy and society we are all trying to build, as well as a national job evaluation scheme.

The first cannot be arrived at without major constitutional changes leading to a new political settlement, while the second raises the spectre of ever more Socialist intervention.

Here the wheel has come full circle to what Keynes said about

1 Institute of Economic Affairs Occasional Paper No. 46 'Employment, Inflation and Politics'.

employment. Full employment, he said, was not a natural state. There was no reason to suppose, as the classical economists had supposed, that the decisions of millions of consumers about their level of consumption, and of hundreds of thousands of businessmen about their level of investment, should just happen to add up to full employment. It was much more likely that they would not do so and that mass employment would result, not for a short time, but for ever.

So today it is ridiculous to suppose that millions of such diverse people making their own decisions will just happen to arrive at stable prices. A stable price level is no more the natural state of things in a modern economy than is full employment. Each has to be worked at, and if not by Government, then by whom?

John Pardoe M.P.

A RECORD OF INFLATION

Michael Jefferson

A RECORD OF INFLATION

Introduction

In recent years inflation has come to be associated with incompetent governments pursuing over-ambitious spending plans; prostrating themselves before powerful but not necessarily representative pressure groups; and resorting to the printing-press as a result of their extravagance, weakness and folly. This state of affairs, it is often remarked, has come to pass not because politicians have become more venal or bureaucrats more anxious to build up empires; rather that these inherent characteristics have, for the past four decades, been given an extra justification and persuasive rationale by Keynesianism.

Looking at the history of inflation, however, the reader is led to question whether inflation can persuasively be set at the door of Keynes (or, more properly, those of his followers keener to expand public expenditure without regard for the resulting pressure to expand the prevailing supply of money). The notion that trade union restrictive practices are the prime cause of inflation becomes at best transitory, because wage demands so obviously excessive are a very recent phenomenon; and may arguably be the consequence of price, tax and a variety of non-economic pressures in a changing socio-political environment. While the so-called monetarist controversy, between what is termed the Chicago School – which is said to argue that there would be no inflation if central governments and banks did not cause the supply of money to increase faster than real output – and its opponents, loses some of its force. Not that the Chicago School represents a monolithic stance, for its doyen (Professor Milton Friedman) often recognizes the strength of forces acting on the monetary authorities and the uncertainties of pursuing restrictive monetary policies to an extent which some of his followers overlook. Indeed, other leading economists, such as Professor Hayek, who often find themselves in sympathy with monetarists outside the field of monetarism, have fundamental differences of view on the causes of inflation. The important point here is that even in the absence of a central administration or a central bank, inflation has often occurred.

What history teaches us, I think, is that inflation generally – but not always – takes place during periods of marked socio-political turbulence, of military strife or of class warfare. Such turbulence often has an adverse effect on agricultural output, and thus exacerbates the consequences of bad harvests. The role of monetary policy is usually significant, and has become increasingly so, if only because undue expansion of the money supply has a permissive effect for the operation of other forces. The role of fiscal policy may also be important, high taxes down the ages have been associated sooner or later with an increasing tax burden on the poorer members of society with inevitable consequences for social discontent.

Above all, inflation can come about from a variety of causes; even a quite temporary imbalance between supply and demand for a particularly significant good or service can spark off an inflationary spiral. Normally however, and there is a great deal of purpose and beauty in the market mechanism even to those who might jib at describing it as 'an invisible hand', these imbalances quite quickly rectify themselves. The great inflations of history have occurred because the very visible hand of military man, or banking man, or vote-catching man, or just plain foolish man has intruded and has not been immediately withdrawn.

In what follows the author has attempted to cover those periods of inflation which seem most significant to him, citing those features which seem of the greatest economic, social or political interest. That such a vast subject can never be covered comprehensively, let alone within the compass of the present essay or by the present writer, is self-evident.

Inflation in Ancient Times

Because inflation has its origins in an imbalance between supply and demand, it follows that the history of inflation arguably stretches back further than the history of money and must be as old as the history of barter. The relative prices of goods exchanged by bartering expressed in the varying quantity of goods that could be exchanged over time for a fixed quantity of other goods, would surely have changed (though this is not strictly inflation). The interest and significance of inflation begins to intensify as money is introduced as a means of exchange and store of value, particularly stable metal forms of money rather than sea shells or blocks of salt or whatever. By 1000 B.C. coins were being used in India and, according to Herodotus, coins had been introduced into the Kingdom of Lydia (part of Turkey) by the eighth century B.C. From there they spread to the Greek cities and their colonies, presumably more swiftly than the fact that few Greek coins have been found on Near Eastern sites before 480 B.C. would suggest.[1]

The first interesting record of inflation occurs in Greece of the fourth century B.C. After the Peloponnesian War there was a succession of wars lasting right through the fourth century, repeated political and social revolutions accompanied them, and regular shortages of food coincided with exaggerated complaints about excessive numbers of mouths to be fed. The mass of the population found their social status in decline, unemployment rose, and what Rostovtzeff has termed 'a true class-war' existed.[2] The situation was exacerbated by an increase in the number of coins in circulation, to an extent far outrunning any increase in production, and the only beneficiaries then – as so often since – appear to have been political leaders who were enriched and bankers whose activities were facilitated.

With the succession of Alexander, however, a period of greater prosperity was ushered in. Although the minting of coins during his reign outran the growth of output the resulting inflation has generally been ascribed more to demand-pull pressures than to the profligacy of those responsible for the issue of coins. In particular, a major famine led to the usual charges of speculation with a number of speculators, Cleomenes of Naucratis in the van, being vilified in the tradition handed down to the 'property-speculator' of our own day.

Under Alexander's successors inflation continued to occur in violent but short-lived spasms, due more to bouts of political chaos than the inadequacies of monetary policy. Coins had by this time become an important symbol of political unity, used as such by Alexander to reinforce his Empire.

More enduring inflation occurred in Ptolemaic Egypt. There successive regimes pursued an independent monetary policy, imposed a vast array of heavy taxes, introduced a proliferating number of monopolies in the provision of staple commodities (which charged excessive prices), and suffered intense social discontent and violence as a result. In order that such thoroughly disliked policies might the more successfully be imposed in an inflationary era the bureaucracy expanded, tax farmers joined and checked upon tax collectors, informers were encouraged, and house searches were carried out. A pattern not unfamiliar in these dark days.

Prices in Egypt continued to rise into the Christian era. Thus the average price of corn quintupled between the beginning of the first-century A.D. and the third century A.D., but from having varied between 12 and 20 drachmae per artaba in the first-half of the third century it rose to about 1,200 drachmae in the time of Diocletian.[3]

This was the situation throughout the Roman Empire which led to Diocletian's Price Edict in A.D. 301. This Edict, apparently promulgated only in the eastern part of the Empire, attempted to stabilize prices by stipulating maximum levels and provided a long tabulation of prices and wages which is unique in ancient price evidence but probably not wholly reliable. However, even if the price ceilings caused goods to be driven off the market because they were too low, as claimed by Lactantius, they showed inter alia that the price of wheat had risen at least 50 fold since a century earlier. But even this price looked low by A.D. 335 when a price 63 times higher than that given in the Edict was quoted on a papyrus.[4]

Before the third century A.D. inflation under the Roman Empire appears to have been very modest. Pay for the Roman legionary, which may have lagged inflation for it appears to have risen in only two substantial steps over the period, rose at a compound rate of under 0.4% per year between 31 B.C. and 200 A.D. In the last three quarters of the third century A.D. prices seem to have risen at a compound rate of 5% per year if averaged throughout the period, although presumably there were bouts of inflation towards the end of the century very much steeper than that.

The reasons for this state of affairs are fascinating, and provide some interesting parallels with current circumstances. There may be some doubts as to whether the fact that the Roman Empire, by the end of the third century A.D., had suffered intensifying external attacks and frequent internal strife between rival emperors (for example, Britain later experienced the usurpation by Constantine III, who crossed the English Channel leaving the country wide open to Saxon invasion) has close modern parallels. More relevant was the growth of bureaucracy.

First, there was an army which though no more numerous in total than Louis XIV had to defend a single Roman province – as Gibbon was to point out – was increasingly found to be beyond the capacity of the Empire to bear. It was not merely that the soldiery required wages and pensions and land in retirement (a resource increasingly difficult to provide as the Empire crumbled at its edges) or that, as Probus's biographer complained, they required compulsory gifts from the populace and oppressed the state with civil wars. They joined others in imposing fierce burdens on and policing the civilian population, depriving people of their possessions and status. Thus Aurelius Eclectus complained in Asia Minor to the Emperor Philip:

> We are most atrociously oppressed and squeezed by those whose duty it is to protect the people. These men – officers, soldiers, city notables holding authority, and your subordinate agents – come to our village and take us away from our work and requisition our plough-oxen, exacting from us what is not due to them, so that we are suffering no ordinary injustice and extortion.

Not only did the bureaucracy proliferate and impose heavy, and often illegal burdens, but they also bound an increasing number of others to the task of working for the state. In the widening immiseration and proletarianisation which resulted, the honest and only moderately prosperous suffered most.

A second feature was the decline in agricultural and more general productivity, the growing area of land left to waste, depopulation and emigration. Productivity declines were in part the result of military conflict, whether external attack or civil strife, and in part due to the requisitioning of labour by the state. Land left to waste was often the result of driving the owner into bankruptcy by heavy taxation and requisitioning of labour, forcing him to flee, or causing him to become a member of a local council and imposing a multiplicity of costs upon him. Depopulation arose because of civil strife, banditry and war, or because of the effects of plague rendered more severe by lack of prosperity and proper nourishment.

'Waste land and state land became gradually synonymous',

Rostovtzeff remarked, and 'the decay of the land was due to the disappearance of private initiative and careful private management.'[5] A list of questions addressed to an Oracle in Fayum Province in the late third century is illuminating. They included:

> 'Shall I be sold up?'
> 'Is my property to be sold by auction?'
> 'Am I to become a beggar?'
> 'Shall I take flight?'
> 'Shall I become an envoy?'
> 'Am I to become a member of the municipal council?'
> 'Shall my flight come to an end?'
> 'Shall I receive my salary?', etc..

We are assured that these questions are typical, they will certainly strike a responsive chord in the ears of the English middle-classes.

Such questions were merely an illustration of the general process whereby a cumulative depression in the status of the lower classes among the free citizens occurred. Later the private contractor and the merchant were eliminated from a considerable sector of the economy,[6] and eventually the elite 'finally responded by retiring to their estates into a condition of maximum self-sufficiency.'[7] This was the response of the people to a burden which by Justinian's reign was estimated to result in the state taking between a quarter and one-third of the gross yield of the Empire, to which must be added the sums diverted beforehand to a host of tax-collectors and officials by way of legal perquisites (the *sportulae*) and illegal exactions. Professor Finley has pointed out with regard to the tax burden:

> The increasing requirements can be attributed in the first instance to that iron law of absolutist bureaucracy that it grows both in numbers and in the expensiveness of its life-style. From the imperial court down, there were, decade by decade, more men to support from public funds, at a steadily growing standard of luxury.[8]

This bureaucracy, and especially the army, were opposed to the bourgeoisie; the bourgeoisie were unwilling to open their ranks to the peasantry, the *humiliores*; the army by the time of Marcus Aurelius and Commodus was largely an army of peasants fully aware, after the usurpation of Septimius, of its power. From a mood of dull submissiveness the attitude of the peasantry became one of hatred and envy towards the privileged classes, not to be wholly assuaged by bread and circuses. Inevitably the wishes of the peasantry, or at least the peasant army, were eventually met but with violence – under the rule of Maximinius and Gallienus. The country was said to have gained a victory over the oppressive city, and Rostovtzeff claimed that the antagonism between the city and the country was the main driving force of the social revolution of the third century A.D.

In fact, despite the sufferings of the bourgeoisie the peasants had gained virtually nothing – and no longer perceived their interests as synonymous with those of the army. They cried out for the stable conditions which were now seen on all sides to be preferable to anarchy. Not only had industry and commerce been decimated within the Empire, but outside it also. Due in part to currency depreciation and in part to the loss of initiative and drive among businessmen, commercial relations with outside territories almost completely ceased. Virtually no coins of the third century have been found in India, for instance, and business relations were not to be resumed until order and a stable currency were re-established in the Byzantine period. Not even the bankers always profited by the inflation – there were cases of banks closing their doors and refusing to deal in imperial currency, with the strikers only succumbing to the direst threats. The bureaucrats once again seemed to be the main beneficiaries of this inflationary period.

In these circumstances it is hardly surprising that Diocletian's stabilization measures were widely accepted, even if they brought no significant improvement to the lot of most people in the Empire. But the reorganisations and reforms of Diocletian, Constantine and their successors – though claiming to cover the army, the bureaucracy and the taxation system – achieved nothing significant. Violence and dishonesty continued and intensified. A mood of resignation spread across that part of the population which would have striven in the circumstances to improve their lot: why improve your land or business, why put in more work, if that meant promotion to the position of a *curialis* which would involve slavery, oppression and ruin? Why succeed in a commercial enterprise, if only to become a member of one of the corporations – the navicularii or mercatores – and work for a miserable pittance for the state?

Material improvement and social advancement became impossible for the honest. But as Rostovtzeff put it:

> The foundation of the new fortunes was no longer the creative

> energy of men, nor the discovery and exploitation of new sources of wealth, nor the improvement and development of commercial, industrial, and agricultural enterprises; it was in the main the skilful use of a privileged position in the state to cheat and exploit the state and the people alike. Public officials, both high and low, grew rich on bribery and corruption.[9]

Nothing, apparently, could reverse the course of decline on which the Empire was set. A political and social process of levelling-down coincided with this decline. Faith in the currency could not be restored, and the fourth century A.D. saw a major shift to payments in kind.

The Mediaeval Period

Inflation continued into the era of the Byzantine Empire, until the early seventh century, after which period (the reign of Heraclius) the principal coin – the nomisma or bezant – kept its value for some five hundred years. Not until about 1200 A.D., following successive debasements, did its prestige decline.

In the Western part of the old Roman Empire no such stability was evident. The Emperor Charlemagne introduced a silver denarius but that quickly became debased. About the same time, in England, Offa was concerned in the issue of a new type of currency, the silver penny or sterling, which continued to form the basis of English currency until long after the Norman Conquest. Because it had not suffered as much from debasement as other coins in Western Europe of the time, this English penny became an international currency with the revival of trade in the eleventh and twelfth centuries.[10]

But the fact that coins retained their intrinsic value or were debased is a poor proxy for the absence or presence of inflation. The role and significance of money in this period has itself been questioned.[11] While such spasmodic evidence as prices going up in about 970 A.D. in Lombardy due to an increase in coins in circulation has limited value. In the absence of price series one is bound to conclude from other evidence – demographic pressures exacerbated by low agricultural productivity (temporarily relieved by improved methods at the beginning of the second millenium), widespread military conflict, uncertain administration – that inflation existed and was often intense.

As the later mediaeval period is approached, so the price data improve – especially for England. Thus between 1208 and 1305 agricultural prices were subject to quite violent fluctuations in response to harvests and the inability to store much of the produce, while the secular trend was steadily upwards. Indeed, the price rise seems to have begun in the mid-eleventh century and, with the average price of grain nearly trebling between the third quarter of the twelfth century and the first quarter of the thirteenth, this period has been described as representing the most violent movement of prices in English history. By 1320 grain prices were four times what they had been in 1180.[12]

Perhaps the most interesting aspect of this whole period is the seeds of peasant protest it contains, protest which was to surface so remarkably in the fourteenth century as a result of inflationary pressures and related causes. The earliest elements, which link the period to the Roman Empire preceding it, were the efforts by peasants to devote as much time as possible to the cultivation of their holding and retain as much of their product as they could, against the competing claims of the state and local rulers. From such movements demands for enfranchisement, local self-government, and the reduction of tax burdens were a natural evolution. Henri Pirenne's statement on the revolt of maritime Flanders in the late fourteenth century, that it was 'a class war between the peasants and the nobility', holds true in general for this period.[13] Significantly, too, production for the market, and the development of commerce and urbanisation, were particularly important in assisting individual freedom and social advancement.

The weights to be placed upon the many factors inducing the peasant revolts of the fourteenth century cannot be applied with any precision. The gains in agricultural productivity had lost much of their impact by the early thirteenth century in relation to the pressure of population, yet before the main revolts the successive plagues of which the Black Death is the most notorious had by the 1370s reduced the population by over one-third.

Increasing tax burdens were another factor. The acceptability of a tax depends in part upon ability to pay and in part upon its conformity with past custom. It was not merely the peasantry that suffered from the consequences of low productivity (a problem which seems to have been exacerbated by a secular deterioration in the climate from the second decade of the thirteenth century), for the real value of money rents in most of Western Europe fell steadily through the thirteenth century. By the end of the century, when population pressures had caused land to become scarcer and its price to go up, rents on hereditary tenancies remained extremely low. English records show that in many parts of the country sales values of wool and grain had risen faster than rental income during the second half of the century, although any conclusions drawn from this situation need qualifying.[14] There were widespread doubts as to whether new tax burdens conformed to earlier practices and were in line with the traditional status and rights of those taxed. And there were doubts, for instance derived from the decline in the rate of fines levied by the manor courts during the thirteenth century, as to the peasants ability to pay.

In maritime Flanders an indemnity tax imposed by the King of France, to be collected by officials of the Count of Flanders, pushed the peasants and the artisans into rebellion in 1379. The Jacquerie uprising in France in 1358 was provoked by the requisitions imposed by the nobility in the Paris region. In Central France taxation imposed by the Duc de Berry in the name of the King of France provoked the Jacquerie of the Tuchins. Extra demands by the Catalonian nobility on the remensas, or servile peasants, for the payment of malos usos provoked their risings (beginning in the 1380s, these spluttered on until the late fifteenth century). In England fiscal pressures had been steadily increasing for a long time, and these sharply intensified in the period 1377 to 1380 and bore down most heavily on the poorest members of society. The Peasants Revolt of 1381 was not a surprising result.

Nevertheless, the secular trend was more advantageous to the peasantry than the reaction to increasing tax burdens might suggest. Between the beginning of the thirteenth century and the middle of the fifteenth century agricultural prices fell about 10 per cent, whereas cash wages had risen two-and-a-half times and real wages had nearly doubled. Harvest work in the years 1371-1380 paid more than double that of the years just before the plague. In general it appears that agricultural and artisans' wages rose by over 50 per cent in money terms between 1350 and 1400, with substantial real increases occurring after 1376.

Other forces involved could be greatly multiplied. The situation in England is of particular interest as the records are unusually good. By the mid-fourteenth century administrative and judicial pressures were intensifying alongside fiscal ones to make the lot of the poor worse. The severe plagues between 1349 and the 1370s had added to the list of grievances, for there had been a rapid seigneurial reaction against efforts by tenants and others to take advantage of the changed land-labour ratio (in some parts of Europe land owners imposed additional taxes in kind on the survivors to make up for lost rental income). Even so, agricultural and other workers demanded up to twice or even three times their previous wages as an almost immediate result of the Black Death, and this led to the wage controls set out in the Ordinance of 1349 and the Statute of Labourers of 1351.[15] One result in the first decade after the Statute's enactment was that labourers, through their fines, were paying one-third to one-half of the total tax burden.

It is particularly regrettable in a record of inflation that little reliable evidence exists on the monetary influences at work. There is scattered information on wages and wheat prices (for example, wheat prices at Exeter from 1316 to 1820), but the sort of historical information produced by Thorold Rogers, or Lord Beveridge's team, or Professor Phelps Brown and Miss Hopkins, tells us little about monetary policy. Nevertheless, there are scraps of evidence which suggest that monetary policy and the monetary system were among the causes of inflation at this time, although not always perceived by contemporaries.[16]

A notable example was Philippe le Bel's prior announcement of a 39 per cent devaluation of the currency in 1306, which caused such a furore in Paris that prices shot up, creditors demanded payment at the new rate, and debts and house rents tripled overnight. Attacks were made on the residences of the Master of the Mint and the King in consequence. Despite these events, further currency devaluations followed in quick succession and provoked satirical verses. In Venice, between 1343 and 1354, there was enormous inflation and currency debasement. In England the two periods of intense inflation during the fourteenth century, one prior to the decade of price stability just before the Black Death (c. 1310-1334) and one just after (c. 1351-1376), are now generally regarded as having been monetary in origin – mainly the result of the exigencies of war finance.[17] While at regular intervals from the late fourteenth century and through the fifteenth century there were references to monetary instability, speculation and hoarding – often as a result of armed conflict. Under these circumstances there was in many districts a revival of barter and payment in kind, and indeed it has been claimed that barter remained the general rule over enormous areas between the fifteenth and the eighteenth centuries.[18] Certainly the period from the twelfth century to the sixteenth century appears to have been remarkable for the extent to which the currency was debased in most of Western Europe. In England, however, the fifteenth century appears to have been a period of reasonable price stability – except for brief bouts of inflation in the 1440s and 1480s – and price rises did not begin in earnest again until after 1518.

The Sixteenth Century Price Revolution

Whether we should describe the inflation of the sixteenth and early seventeenth centuries as a 'price revolution', when it appears mild compared with some earlier standards and with recent experience, the description has gained general acceptance since Georg Wiebe coined it in 1895.[19]

The bare facts on inflation in the sixteenth century are fairly simply told (although the data can only sustain very broad statements). In England food prices rose almost five-fold between 1500 and 1600 (non-agricultural prices rose much less sharply).[20] This compares with a quadrupling of food prices in England during the 120 years preceding the early fourteenth century, and the nearly ten-fold general price increase so far this century.[21] In Spain, food prices increased about five-fold between 1500 and 1600 (although other studies by Earl J. Hamilton suggested the increase might be nearer four-fold).[22] But food prices in France, Poland (Krakow), and – more particularly – Germany (Frankfurt), Italy and Sweden rose even less rapidly. Thus Professor Cipolla has shown that prices did not start rising in Italy until the mid-sixteenth century, and that although an inflation rate of 5.2 per cent per annum was achieved between 1552 and 1560 prices only doubled between 1552 and 1600 – a simple average annual increase of 2 per cent.

Three problems immediately present themselves, however. First, whereas the marked rise in food prices indicates the sort of inflation just quoted, in fact the prices of most non-agricultural products do not exhibit such a marked upward trend. The prices of building materials, metals, textiles and other manufactures, and goods imported from newly-acquired overseas territories, rose but a fraction of agricultural prices.[23] Second, the commencement of this so-called price revolution varies markedly between countries. In

England it begins after 1518, in Spain after 1513, in other countries it begins up to forty years later or barely at all. Both these points are relevant to the third problem, what were the factors which caused this rise in prices?

The rise of food prices through the century after 1515 is a first indication that intensifying population pressures were an important factor in the renewed and increasing inflation in England. The rise in population appears to have been most marked in the first half of the century for thereafter later marriages, smaller families and the ravages of influenza epidemics from 1556 exerted a downward pressure.[24] Prices showed a similar pattern for most of the century, the rate of increase slowing from the 1560s to the 1580s before a further rapid rise began in the 1590s.

The impact of population pressures was exacerbated by the slow rise of agricultural productivity both absolutely and in relation to rises in industrial productivity. This is a phenomenon which has been noted and stressed in subsequent inflationary periods.[25] Other 'real' forces at work included the expensive military campaigns against the Scots and the French in the 1540s, and against Spain and Ireland in the 1590s; the 'rackynge and hoyssing up of Rentes' as Sir Thomas Smith picturesquely put it, for which Dr Eric Kerridge is now the leading exponent; and a pot-pourri of less persuasive arguments such as excessive exports (forerunner of the overseas direct investment controversy of recent years?); the activities of monopolies (forerunner of the arguments against large firms in concentrated industries and multinational corporations?); and the speculations of middlemen (forerunners of the property speculators and other like targets of recent years?).

But after the combined effects of population pressure and inadequate rises in agricultural productivity, the main cause of inflation appears to have been monetary (the respective weights to be attached to these causes cannot, of course, be judged with precision). The two main monetary forces at work were debasement of the coinage and importation of bullion.

Debasement of the coinage was an early explantion for inflation in sixteenth-century England, appearing in Sir Thomas Smith's 'Discourse of the Common Weal' (1549) as the main cause of price increases in the preceding few years. On balance it would seem that the great debasement period, 1544-1551, did have a marked impact both psychological and real as J.D. Gould has stressed.[26] Nevertheless, there is a dissenting view: that the effects of debasement were largely confined to the latter part of the debasement period; people in general were not very sensitive to it; and that debasement occurred at a time of severe shortage of specie and thus had only a modest effect on prices.[27]

More important in the broader context is that with prices rising in England from the second decade of the sixteenth-century, as they were in Spain, the relevance of a debasement commencing thirty years later is doubtful. This is one of the reasons why inflow of New World bullion to Spain, percolating elsewhere, was such a popular explanation of the sixteenth-century price revolution in the late nineteenth and early twentieth centuries – following the work of James Thorold Rogers and Earl J. Hamilton. Although the connection seems fairly clear for Spain, there are difficulties both of timing and causation for England.

As to timing, bullion imports into Spain from the New World began to rise rapidly only in the late 1530s, when inflation had been intensifying in England for the previous two decades. It is indeed interesting that contemporaries were slow to advance the bullion inflow hypothesis, perhaps the earliest published case in English being the 1581 edition of Smith's 'Discourse of the Common Weal', probably influenced by Jean Bodin's treatise of 1568. However, the qualification as to timing is modified by the fact that silver production in Europe rapidly increased from the late fifteenth century, especially in Germany and Bohemia, causing inflationary pressures on the Continent and peaking in the decade 1525-1535.[28]

But how was this bullion transmitted to England in such quantities as to stoke up powerful inflationary pressures, or how did this bullion indirectly have such an impact on English prices? The difficulties are not insuperable, but the activities of men like Drake or Mary Tudor's receipt of a dowry from Spain cannot loom large in the chain of causation. Moreover, if substantial inflows had occurred this might have been expected to have a depressing effect on gold and silver prices, which did not occur. It seems in fact that the market for money and the market for precious metals operated fairly independently of one another.[29]

Elsewhere in Europe population appeared to be growing through the century, although most of the evidence comes from larger towns and there was considerable immigration from rural areas to the towns. Even where it is considered that a general population increase was occurring, such as in many of the Mediterranean countries,[30] we know that sustained inflation did not always follow.

In Spain, the rate of price increase was faster in the first-half of the sixteenth century, when bullion imports were building up, than in the second-half when bullion was flooding in. This is not to deny Earl J. Hamilton's famous conclusion: 'Among the causes of the price revolution in Andalusia there can be no doubt that the greatest was the influx of American treasure', particularly given his rider that many other factors were at work.[31] Rather, it is impossible to gauge how much more important the bullion imports were than other inflationary forces at work – individually or in aggregate.

The Seventeenth Century

One of the problems of fixing firm time periods to historical phenomena is that events have a habit of failing to conform to such a Procrustean bed. Thus the sixteenth-century price revolution did not end in the year 1600, but continued with little abatement in several European countries until the middle of the seventeenth century.

In England, prices peaked around 1650 at a level not far short of double that of half a century earlier. Nor could civil strife and uncertain administration be blamed for much of this increase, for prices in 1650 were only one-third up on those prevailing in the late 1630s. Prior to that, downward pressure on real incomes had once again been accompanied by rising burdens of taxation. It was not until the 1770s that the mid-seventeenth-century price levels were to be achieved again, because a century of fluctuating but broadly stable prices followed the Civil War and persistent inflation did not recommence until the late 1750s.

On the Continent, the situation was also characterized by socio political instability, notably in Spain. As Earl J. Hamilton put it: 'It took Spain only a century (from the union of Castile and Aragon, in 1479, to the annexation of Portugal, in 1580) to attain political pre-eminence and only a century (from the death of Philip II, in 1598, to that of Charles II, in 1700) to fall into the rank of a second-rate power.'[32] As in so many cases of the decline of empires, economic weakness combined with an over-burgeoning bureaucracy, public corruption, crushing tax-burdens, a disinclination for hard work, and spasmodic military ventures which ended in failure. Spain's problems and decline were recognised early on, as early as 1600, by the Arbitristas but to no effect. To economic weakness in agriculture and manufacturing, depopulation, and the consequences of expelling the Moriscos, was added a powerful monetary influence. It was no coincidence that the vellon, a coin of silver and copper mixed, had a declining proportion of silver which disappeared entirely in 1599. Various attempts to restore the silver were ineffectual. Another silver coin, the real, had its silver content reduced by one-quarter in 1642.

Copper was becoming more significant in coinage after 1600, but with the beginnings of exhaustion in the American mines around 1620, the end of the silver era was in sight. By the 1640s the circulation of specie had plummeted, exchange was hampered, and 'the copper revolution' saved the situation. However, incautious minting of copper coinage was, of course, inflationary. From 1599 to 1628 severe inflationary pressures were caused in large part by the minting of millions of copper vellon coins (moderated between 1608 and 1617 by prohibition of such minting).

Effective deflationary measures were introduced in 1628 but had broken down by 1634, and inflation recurred at an increasing rate until there was a huge inflationary crisis in 1641. The vellon had been devalued by 50 per cent in 1628. In 1636 its face value was tripled. The 4-maravedi coin had its face value doubled in February, 1641; the 2-maravedi coin, and 4-maravedi coins minted after 1603 (when earlier coins had been restamped), had their face value tripled in October, 1641. Silver fetched a premium of 190 per cent by August, 1642. In the deflation carried out at the end of 1642 coins were brutally reduced in face value, the 12-maravedi and 6-maravedi coins to one-sixth of their former value. However, military ventures in Milan and Flanders obliged Philip IV to reverse the deflationary process, and in 1651 the 2-maravedi coin had its nominal value quadrupled and new copper coins weighing only one-quarter of the old coins were minted in profusion.

Further debasement occurred in 1654, and the 2-maravedi coin was doubled in nominal value again in 1658. Within a few months further deflationary measures were attempted, but with little effect. Through the 1660s and 1670s the situation went from bad to worse. The silver premium has risen from 50 per cent in 1650 to 150 per cent in 1660, to 120 per cent in 1665, and to 180 per cent in 1669. After stabilizing in the early 1670s, the premium rose to 275 per cent in 1679, on the eve of the Great Crash of 1680. Deflationary action in the latter year was followed within a few months by a 45 per cent drop in wholesale prices (as bad as anything in 1919/1920 or 1929/34) and disaster ensued. By 1686 the situation had restablized, much of the copper had been withdrawn from circulation, silver had been revalued, and gold had begun to flow in from Brazil.[33]

These monetary fluctuations were more intense in Andalucia than they were in Valencia, more marked in Spain than they were in the rest of Continental Europe. In France, for instance, inflation was more or less persistent from 1602 until the stabilization measures of Louis XV in 1726. But French coinage, after a 30 per cent drop in metallic content during the Thirty Years War, stayed broadly unchanged between 1602 and 1640, and between 1644 and 1689. In Italy prices tended to fall for much of the seventeenth century, particularly for manufactured goods, despite steady devaluation. Thus between 1620 and 1700 the silver content of the Genoese lira fell by about 30 per cent, of the Milanese lira by 20 per cent, and of the Venetian lira by 15 per cent.[34]

On the whole, however, inflation was modest or absent between 1650 and 1750 in much of Europe. Castile was a notable exception, and particularly in times of military strife there were bouts of inflation elsewhere.

The Eighteenth Century

Although the first six decades of the eighteenth century were characterized by marked price stability, this is not to say that fluctuations did not occur. There were frequent financial crises, and the beginnings of the modern banking system in England and growth of paper assets were marked with turbulence. On the Continent monetary turbulence regularly rippled out from such financial centres as Hamburg and Amsterdam coinciding with military expeditions or peace, speculative frenzy or natural disasters.[35]

In England, however, prices did not start to rise again until the late 1750s or early 1760s – a period of inflation and financial crisis which was to recur in the early 1770s. By the 1790s prices were in general more than a third higher than those prevailing in the first decade of the century.[36] This was the run-up to the Napoleonic Wars which, like the First and Second World Wars, had a marked inflationary impact. Real wages in general appeared to keep pace with this upward drift of prices through to the close of the Napoleonic Wars, however, and in the North of England and Scotland seem to have risen faster from the mid-eighteenth century.[37]

In North America the excessive issue of paper money was early on blamed for inflation. By the middle of the eighteenth century notes had declined to one-tenth of their corresponding value in gold or silver of fifty years before. But it was not until the War of Independence that inflation really took off. By 1777 it was said that 'a wagon-load of money would scarcely purchase a wagon-load of provisions'. In Virginia shoes cost $5000 per pair in local notes, and a set of clothing at least $1 million. Debtors sought to repay their debts in worthless notes, and creditors hid from them. Widows left with a substantial inheritance found themselves worth nothing. But for the whole mythology surrounding the struggle for independence this period would be looked upon with the same horror as is accorded to Weimar Germany or, as we shall now see, Revolutionary France. For within two decades of the events just described was to come one of the most spectacular and interesting periods of inflation, that which accompanied the issue of assignats – paper money – in the years 1790 to 1797. The story was told long ago in a remarkable paper by Andrew Dickson White.[38]

It was not the first time in eighteenth century France that people were shown to have been credulous in their acceptance of paper money. John Law's activities between 1716 and 1720 were another remarkable example.[39] But in May, 1789 Louis XVI had called a meeting of the States-General in an attempt to tackle the bankruptcy of the public treasury, the major step in the final road to Revolution. Over the next few months pressure built up to chance a short-cut out of the financial mess, despite some dissenting voices which based their view on previous experience, and in April, 1790 came the decree to issue 400 million livres of paper money. This sum was issued in assignats, notes secured by a pledge of productive land and bearing interest to the holder of 3 per cent per annum. The National Assembly informed the nation that it had been 'delivered by this grand means from all uncertainty and from all ruinous results of the credit system'. The issue 'would bring back into the public treasury, into commerce, and into all branches of industry strength, abundance, and prosperity'.

The immediate consequences were, as so often before and since, encouraging as trade revived and the public debt was reduced. But, within five months of the assignats being first issued, the government had spent them and was again in distress. At the end of September, 1790 a further 800 million assignats were decreed to be issued, Mirabeau leading the call for further inflation on political grounds while privately thinking that 'that infamous word, paper money, ought to be banished from our language'. More and smaller notes were issued; silver, gold and copper became scarce despite the King sending in his gold and silver plate for minting – as did the churches with spare gold and silver vessels, and with their copper bells. Prices were spiralling upwards, specie was disappearing as bad money drove out good, enterprise was undermined and business stagnated.

Despite the inevitable consequences of this monetary inflation, assignats continued to be issued in larger and larger amounts. A third issue of 600 million took place in June, 1791; a fourth issue of 300 million in December, 1791; a fifth of 300 million in April, 1792; a sixth of 300 million in the summer of 1792. The number of assignats in circulation rose from 3,000 million livres in early 1793 to 4,200 million in early 1794; to 14,000 million in early 1795; and to 40,000 million in February, 1796, when the machinery, plates and paper for printing assignats were destroyed. A year later, in February, 1797 both assignats and their more modest successor – the mandat – ceased to be legal tender.

Long before the end of this process industry and commerce had collapsed and mass unemployment had been caused. Wages suffered; dishonesty, gambling and speculation grew. Debtors had an interest in encouraging inflation, in order to reduce their burdens, creditors increasingly saw that thrift in such circumstances was useless. The debtor who had borrowed 10,000 francs in 1790 could repay it with 35 francs in 1796. People lost their inheritances, money set aside for childrens' education or retirement was worth nothing, debt stabilization schemes came to nought.[40] The parallels with Weimar Germany are self-evident. Then came forced loans through new taxes; price and profit controls through the Law of the Maximum of September, 1793; and a powerful undercurrent of violence directed at all and sundry throughout, as mob rule and personal antagonisms together did their bloody work.

As in Germany of the Weimar Republic, there was a measure of the inflation which was taking place. The louis d'or of 25 francs was already worth 920 paper francs by August, 1795; 1200 paper francs by the following September; 2600 francs by November, and 3,050 francs by the beginning of December. In February, 1796 it was worth 7,200 paper francs and eventually was worth 15,000 francs before assignats ceased to be legal tender. Prices rose more or less in proportion. Thus flour costing 2 francs in 1790 cost 225 francs in 1795; a pair of shoes costing 5 francs in 1790 cost 200 francs in 1795. A cartload of wood cost 125 times the 1790 price in 1795. Butter cost 560 francs per pound in 1795, a turkey 900 francs. (It is interesting to note how relative prices changed, along lines later to be seen in Weimar Germany).

As in Germany of the early 1920s there arose a few speculators, contractors, and gamblers living in temporary and debauched luxury. Their wives indulged in the most ostentatious extravagance. Tallien was the French equivalent of Hugo Stinnes in Germany 130 years later. Meanwhile, not only did the vast majority of the once wealthy suffer impoverishment, but so did all salaried employees, those on fixed incomes, and the working-classes. Long bread queues formed for government rations which were often unfit for human consumption. The scene was set for a return to stability, propitious for the rise of a dictator, as virtually everyone tired of and turned away from anarchy. So Napoleon arose, not so much like a Phoenix for he was to create many ashes himself, but with a determination – as he put it in his first cabinet council – to pay cash or pay nothing. Even when the first European coalition was formed against him, and he was under pressure to resort to paper money, Napoleon wrote: 'While I live, I will never resort to irredeemable paper'. He never did.

In England prices had been escalating rapidly under pressures of wartime financing and dislocation. Consumer goods virtually doubled in price between 1789 and 1801, consumer goods other than cereals rose two-thirds over the same period, and producers' goods rose about 55 per cent. Prices then fell with the Peace of Amiens in 1802 to a plateau which remained high before peaking again in 1812-1815.

During the Napoleonic Wars several incidents of importance in the history of banking occurred which are worth mentioning here. The failure of the credit of the country banks on France's declaration of war against England in 1793, and the Bank of

England's effective assistance; the Bank's protests against what it deemed excessive Government borrowing, particularly from 1794 to 1796; the Bank's restriction on issuing gold in payment from 1797; the inflation of 1799-1800 when the note issue rose from £12½mn. to £16mn.; and the inflation of 1809-1810 when the note issue rose from £17mn. to over £21mn. by May, 1810. This last incident provoked the creation by the House of Commons of its famous Bullion Committee. Reporting in mid-1810 it was no coincidence that the Committee's conclusions closely resembled those of some articles written in the 'Morning Chronicle' the previous year by Ricardo, that the rise in the price of bullion and depreciation of the currency had been caused solely by an over-issue of Bank of England notes.[41] Opposition to the Committee's report was highly confused, but no less effective for that.

Following Waterloo prices began to fall, dropping about 20 per cent between 1822 and 1851, but so did most wages and this has led to a major debate among historians to which we will return below: what happened to real wages and the general standard of living in England in the first-half of the nineteenth-century?

The second-half of the eighteenth century also saw the decline of the Dutch Empire, although the seeds of decay are discernible from the 1690s and the relative stagnation during the eighteenth century–or Periwig Period–was probably not as severe as some commentators have claimed. It can hardly be claimed that the inflation which occurred from the 1750s to the end of the century, especially in agricultural prices, was the principal cause of this decline. Nevertheless, in urban communities the proliferating and intense tax burdens since the 1690s, together with the loss of seaborne power and those innovative and entrepreneurial qualities so evident in earlier days, had weakened the capacity to bear the further burden of rising prices.[42] Even in rural areas, such as Overijssel Province, where the rise in agricultural prices moderated the effects of taxation the condition of the poor markedly declined.[43]

Elsewhere in Europe the late eighteenth century exhibited much more modest price rises than France or England. In Germany wholesale prices appear to have risen 35 per cent between 1792 and 1801. In Spain wholesale prices appear to have risen little more than 21 per cent between 1789 and 1800, but no reliable data exist for the following decade.[44]

The Nineteenth Century

In the years following the dislocation of the transition from war to peace of 1815 the greatest interest lies neither in inflation nor in the deflation which actually occurred – in large part the consequence of monetary measures – but in what happened to real wages.

The 'standard-of-living controversy' has long been central to the socialist/Marxist tradition in British historiography, which advanced the view that the quality of life certainly declined in the first-half of the century, and the general material standard of living probably declined. This tradition has been opposed, especially over the past half-century, by a succession of able 'optimists'. The left-wing tradition seems, in the perhaps over-optimistic recent words of Professor Peter Mathias, 'to be being driven out of economic history by quantification and the dictates of neo-classical economic theory to find a sympathetic new base in a revitalized social history. Professor Hobsbawn and Mr Edward Thompson are marching off this particular battlefield under a banner which reads 'Thou shalt not judge by real wage indexes alone'. They are concerned with all the non-quantifiable aspects of the way of life which industrialization and urbanization brought with them ...'[45]

The details of this controversy, the qualifications to the optimistic thesis caused by the plight of particular groups of impoverished workers such as handloom weavers or the wide regional disparities, do not concern us here.[46] The significant point is the existence and powerful impact of this tradition firmly embedded not only in left-wing historiography but in High Tory attitudes and a major literary tradition of hostility to industrialization, the factory system, and personal involvement in industry or trade.[47] Such attitudes have increasingly paved the way in Britain (and to some extent in the U.S.A. and other English-speaking countries) for deficit financing of government welfare programmes, increasingly harsh 'progressive' taxation, growing central and local government bureaucracy, the burgeoning encroachment of authority upon individual life and liberty, and erosion of confidence in the capitalist system. There is no way of judging the strength of the various threads in this story, but the continuing strength of the literary and oral tradition as well as the tradition passed down from Toynbee through the Hammonds to E.P. Thompson is neglected at our peril in understanding some of the inflationary forces of recent years.

The fall in prices in England continued from the early 1820s to 1851. Then, as Sir John Clapham put it: 'There can be very little doubt that the marked upward heave of general prices between the triennium 1849-51 and the triennium 1868-70 was closely connected with the great addition to the world's stock of coined and circulating gold, which was accompanied by a growing use of paper money in its various forms'.[48] Prices then renewed their downward drift to the mid-1880s and, after a temporary pause, fell further to the mid-1890s, when they were about 20 per cent below the 1851 level. This price decline was linked with the so-called Great Depression, which though a confused and multi-faceted problem was not quite the myth it has recently been called.[49] From 1896 onwards, however, prices began their rising trend through to the highly inflationary First World War. Yet between 1815 and 1913 the price index had remained remarkable stable, lying between 70 per cent and 120 per cent of the 1913 level. And if the Napoleonic Wars and their immediate aftermath are excluded, prices between 1660 and 1913 fluctuated between one-third above and one-third below the level in the latter year.[50]

On the Continent of Europe prices showed a broadly similar pattern through the nineteenth century. Von Jankovich's work on prices in the Austro-Hungarian Empire suggests wholesale prices fell steadily from the early 1870s to the mid-1890s, so that by 1896 they were only two-thirds the level of 1871. In Germany wholesale prices fell sharply after 1817 until the mid-1820s, and maintained this new low level of about half the prices prevailing in 1817 until the early 1850s. In the early 1860s prices then began their rise to a higher plateau about one-quarter above that of the previous three decades before climbing to a new peak in the early 1870s, after which a decline set in until the mid-1890s in common with much of the rest of Europe. Wholesale prices in Germany by 1894 were, therefore, only two-thirds of the level prevailing twenty years earlier. In Sweden price movements were much the same as in Germany both as to timing and as to size of fluctuation, and the more limited Norwegian evidence points in the same direction.

Among the South European countries, French wholesale prices fell steadily after 1817 until a sharp rise occurred in the early 1850s to levels some 30 per cent higher than had prevailed in 1848-1851 by 1853-54. Steady price decline set in again in the early 1870s until, as elsewhere, the mid-1890s. The price decline was less marked in Italy, levels in the mid-1890s being three-quarters of their peak in 1873-74. In Spain, using Juan Sarda's estimates, wholesale prices appear to have peaked earlier – in the mid-1860s – and reached their new low plateau by the mid-1880s before renewing their upward climb ten years later. But the biggest fluctuation in Spain of the century had already occurred – wholesale prices halved between 1812 and 1820, and were only two-thirds the 1820 level by 1830.

The nineteenth-century also saw the beginnings of Japan's emergence as a major industrial nation. From the 1860s Japan's imperial decline was halted and reversed as the forward-looking, aristocratic authors of the Meiji Restoration created the Tokugawa Shogunate, a rare example of a nation escaping out of the vortex of secular decline. Wholesale prices more than doubled between the late 1880s and 1914, pushed up primarily by domestic monetary and fiscal policies although assisted in the decade before the First World War by rising import prices.[51]

In the United States the most striking feature of the century was the inflation of the Civil War period, with prices peaking in 1864, and the subsequent fall of the general price level to half that of fifteen years before. This was the 'greenback period'.

Prices fell rapidly in the immediate aftermath of the war, in part as the result of deliberate deflationary policy, and were 25 per cent lower by 1867. Then the rate of decline moderated, and there was even a rise between 1871 and 1873, before a further sharp decline between 1876 and 1879. Then from 1879 to mid-1897 prices fell at the rate of 1 per cent per year, before rising at 2 per cent per year from second-half 1897 to 1914 (and wholesale prices rose $2\frac{1}{2}$ per cent per year). Until the post-1945 period, this 40 per cent rise in the general price level (nearer 50 per cent rise in wholesale prices) was unmatched in American history. It was a much more rapid increase than occurred in Europe where, for instance, British wholesale prices rose 26 per cent between 1897 and 1914. A major cause was the greatly increased and more efficient extraction of gold from South Africa, Alaska, and Colorado.[52]

The First World War

We have noted the general rise of prices throughout the western world from the mid-1890s to 1914. This was in part caused by monetary factors, but there were other influences at work. A number of European nations had engaged upon major armaments programmes. Structural changes were taking place, thus in Britain the lure of the large towns seemed less compelling to those in rural areas. And there were institutional forces at work, one of which in Britain, in particular, should be noticed.

The trade union movement in Britain had, until the turn of the century, tended to bolster, or at least not diminish, the existing wide regional differentials in wages. But with the rising power of socialism and working-class political parties, combined with the more extreme activities of a small number of working men and anarchists, pressure built up for a variety of changes. Collective bargaining spread, and across-the-board increases became general, especially during the First World War. These changes were to reinforce the inflationary pressures which excessive wage demands could produce, although much time was to pass and much unemployment and misery before the opportunity arose in earnest.

With the First World War, wholesale prices rose some 7 per cent in the first month, due to a rise in food prices, and then steadied for the remainder of 1914. A further sharp rise followed in the first three months of 1915, and then several more months of stability. But between October, 1915 and May, 1916 wholesale prices rose 28 per cent and then, after a brief fall, rose another 35 per cent between July, 1916 and June, 1917. The reason why the rate of increase slowed was because price controls had been imposed on most of the major items in the index. For the last seventeen months of the war, the wholesale price rise was only 10 per cent. Nevertheless, a price increase of 140 per cent had occurred in the four years of hostilities.[53] This inflation cannot be disassociated from the heightened demand for raw materials and products – but there was lax monetary policy and a great deal of deficit financing by the British Government. The presumption that although the degree of inflation in Britain was less than in many countries 'government financial policy permitted this inflation to occur rather than caused it' therefore seems reasonable.[54]

On the Continent of Europe price rises tended to be larger, although there were wide variations between nations. In Germany and Spain they doubled between 1914 and 1918. In The Netherlands they rose by 1918 to $2\frac{1}{2}$ times their 1914 level; in Norway and Sweden they trebled. In France, Belgium and Italy, prices quadrupled over the period; in Finland they rose more than five-fold; in Czechoslovakia they rose 16-fold; and in Bulgaria they rose even more than that.

In the United States wholesale prices doubled between 1914 and 1918, although general price levels rose rather more slowly. In Japan, which was only technically at war and able to both supply armaments to the belligerents and move in to fulfil the peacetime trading role hitherto performed by others in the Far East, there was substantial pressure on resources and inflationary credit policies. The result was a 150 per cent rise in wholesale prices during the four years' hostilities, the largest rise in prices over such a short period in Japanese history.

But war-time conditions, the pressures on Governments to finance hostilities, the scramble for raw materials, the ability to impose controls on prices and other such emergency measures, provide opportunities for inflation which the most conservative monetary specialists would recognize. And whereas the scale of the First World War was such as to render substantial inflation unavoidable, the massive reduction in price levels after the war in all but one major country did occur on a scale which was surprising.

In Britain, wholesale prices as indicated by the Board of Trade's Wholesale Price Index virtually halved between 1920 (the collapse began in May 1920) and 1922, although the Ministry of Labour's Retail Price Index fell little more than 25 per cent over the same period. The counter-inflationary measures which had been taken to deal with the inflation from 1919 developed into a thorough-going deflationary policy. The Cunliffe Committee of 1918 had advised that a return to the gold standard was desirable and, in order to achieve this at the pre-war parity, British prices had to be brought down to U.S. levels by severe credit restriction. These steps were reinforced when the Geddes Committee on National Expenditure was set up in 1921 to recommend possible cuts in public expenditure, and the 'Geddes Axe' began to be wielded in consequence.

In France wholesale prices fell one-third between 1920 and 1922, and in The Netherlands by nearer 40 per cent (where prices had already fallen 8 per cent between 1919 and 1920). Another 40 per cent fall in wholesale prices was recorded in Norway, while prices halved in Sweden. Similar falls were recorded in the United States, where between May 1920 and June 1921 wholesale prices fell 56 per cent – most of it taking place between August 1920 and February 1921. This seems, despite rapid price falls after the War of 1812 and the Civil War, to have been the sharpest price decline in American history.

There were, however, two exceptions in Western Europe to this general pattern. The first was Italy, where prices continued on a rising trend through the First World War and early post-war years until 1926 before declining. Their level in 1926 was 50 per cent above the level in 1918; nevertheless their decline from 1926 until 1934 was one of the steepest in those years and left Italian prices at half the level of eight years before. The second was Germany where, under the Weimar Republic, the best-known example of hyperinflation this century occurred.

The Great German Inflation of 1923

The onset of this inflation can be traced to before the First World War, in Germany's large military expenditures and laxity of monetary policy which intensified from 1910. During the War itself the extraordinary reliance on borrowing and the small recourse to taxation made intense inflation inevitable, but with the political and social tensions which arose in the wake of defeat – made worse by the curious but widespread belief that democratic politicians had stabbed the army in the back – there was inadequate control over monetary policy at the centre. In addition, the terms of the Treaty of Versailles were regarded as excessively punitive to be met largely by use of the money printing-press. And, initially at least, there seems to have been little enough understanding by central bankers downwards of the consequences of such vast increases in the money supply and total resignation towards the discounting of Government bills.

The bare statistical facts tell their own dismal tale:

Depreciation of the German Mark

Month of analysis	*Measured by*	
	U.S. $1	*Wholesale Prices*
January 1913	4.2	1.0
January 1920	64.8	12.6
July 1920	39.5	13.7
January 1921	64.9	14.4
July 1921	76.7	14.3
January 1922	191.8	36.7
July 1922	493.2	101.0
January 1923	17,972.0	2,785.0
July 1923	353,412.0	74,787.0
August 1923	4,620,455.0	944,041.0
September 1923	98,860,000.0	23,949,000.0
October 1923	25,260,208,000.0	7,095,800,000.0
15th November, 1923	4,200,000,000,000.0	750,000,000,000.0

Currency in circulation increased from 6 billion marks in 1913 to just over 33 billion in 1918, and then rose as follows:

Notes and Coins in Circulation (Billions of Marks)

	1919	50
	1920	82
	1921	123
	1922	1,295
October	1923	2,500,000
November	1923	92,000,000

The face value of mark notes increased correspondingly. In May 1922 the 10,000 mark note made its first appearance. Larger denominations followed, in quick succession during 1923. Finally, the 100 billion mark note made its appearance. This was no more absurd than the detailed entry of the cost of manufacturing these bank notes in the Reichsbank's accounts:

32, 776, 899, 763, 734, 490, 417 marks and 5 pfennigs.

As Rudolf Havenstein ended his address to the Executive Committee of the Reichsbank in August 1923 – in which he rejected claims that the Reichsbank bore a large part of the responsibility for the disorganization of the currency and the increasing inflation:

> The running of the Reichsbank's note printing organisation, which has become absolutely enormous, is making the most extreme demands on our personnel. The dispatching of cash sums must, for reasons of speed, be made by private transport. Numerous shipments leave Berlin every day for the provinces. The deliveries to several banks can be made only by airplanes.

People who owned Government securities, held life insurance policies, or owned mortgaged property were expropriated on a vast scale – and subsequent compensation was derisory. Real wages fell steadily until the beginning of 1923, when they were only half their pre-war level, but then an indexation scheme came into operation. Workers began to receive their pay daily, although even then the value of their pay packets could fall between its receipt and the time it took to cover the short distance to the shops. Salary workers in general were less well protected, and income differentials narrowed markedly. Even if you had money it might not be acceptable to the farmer or shopkeeper. Eggs were exchanged for a hair cut, a sausage for the mending of a pair of shoes, two pieces of coal for entry to a cinema. It was said that if you left a basket full of money unattended you would return to find the basket gone, but the money still there.

William Guttmann has related how, entering a cafe, a cup of coffee cost 5,000 marks. By the time he had finished it, the cost was 8,000 marks.[55] An egg which would have cost 8 pfennigs before the First World War could cost 5,000 marks by the middle of 1923 and 80 billion marks in November 1923. A pair of shoes would have cost 12 marks in 1913, but cost over 1 million marks in the summer of 1923 and 32,000 billion marks in November 1923. Pearl Buck reported an interview with Erna von Pustau, who lived in Hamburg at this time, in 'How It Happens: Talk About the German People, 1914-1933' (1947). Here again, the cost of a couple of bread rolls could go up 25 per cent while you were having lunch. But it was the moral decay which struck people at the time – the spread of bribery and corruption into almost every aspect of life; the decay and collapse of middle-class standards of thrift and honesty; the selling of possessions acquired over a life-time for a little food; the emergence of speculators, spivs, ostentation and vulgarity on the part of those able to scramble up on the backs of others. Savings wiped out, fixed incomes savagely cut, salaries rapidly declining in real worth unless carefully indexed – and even then of reduced value because prices rose by the hour if not by the minute as inflation reached the top of its crescendo in November 1923.[56] The material pressures were but the external indication of the pressures undermining morality, encouraging rancour, sowing the seeds of the horrors which were to develop ten years later. The first results were the sort of immoral or amoral atmosphere which pervades Erich Kästner's novel 'Fabian'.[57] The second, as Stefan Zweig put it: 'Nothing made the German people so embittered, so raging with hatred, so ripe for Hitler, as the Inflation.'

On the other hand, Mr Adam Fergusson, in his recent book on this subject, is surely correct to remind us that the scourge of inflation followed the scourge of defeat in war, and that it is difficult to believe that the psychological trauma of the early 1920's in Germany was solely the result of inflation.[58]

By the middle of November 1923 a number of measures had been introduced or were on the point of introduction, to stabilize the situation. These measures relied in large part upon their psychological impact – after all, two episodes in France in the eighteenth century suggest that linking a bank's capital to charges on the nation's land (to which was now added a charge on its industrial and commercial enterprises) and issuing bonds on the strength of these charges need not halt inflation. But this is what the Germans did with the creation of the Rentenbank and the Rentenmark, skilfully operated by Dr Schacht from a little office. The situation was not righted straight away, the U.S. $1 was worth 11 billion marks in Cologne and not much less in New York on 26 November, 1923, but thereafter the economic situation improved rapidly. The social, political and moral situation was less easily and quickly corrected.

Further to the East – in Austria, Hungary, Poland and Russia – hyperinflation had also occurred. In some cases it had for a time run ahead of inflation in Germany. Thus in Austria £1 had been worth 25 Kronen in 1914, but in May 1922 was worth 35,000 Kronen. This depreciation was slightly worse than that of the German mark up to that time. Inflation had come earlier and had been sharper. Even in the early months of 1919 a Viennese lady noted that although a suit only cost six times its pre-war price, some items of food cost 100 to 200 times more. But by the mid-1920's prices everywhere were falling. A return to the gold-exchange standard of pre-war years, not always at realistic parities (Britain's return to the gold standard in 1925 was at a hopelessly unrealistic parity), reinforced the decline of prices and of incomes. The money stock in many countries held steady or fell and, when a cyclical down-turn occurred in the United States from August 1929, the 'great contraction' in the U.S. money supply reinforced the downturn and had severe repercussions in Europe.[59] The fall in prices continued until 1933/34, by which time the percentage declines from 1929 were:

Austria	—	17%	Italy	—	35%
Belgium	—	44%	Netherlands	—	37%
Bulgaria	—	47%	Poland	—	42%
Czechoslovakia	—	28%	Rumania	—	48%
Denmark	—	17%	Sweden	—	24%
France	—	41%	Switzerland	—	36%
Germany	—	32%	U.K.	—	25%
Hungary	—	39%	U.S.A.	—	36%
			Yugoslavia	—	37%

The only exceptions to this pattern were Spain and Greece in the Western world, where prices remained fairly steady in these years. But after 1934, in response to new or shifting perceptions of the role of Government in economic and social affairs, and to the growing clouds of yet another major war, prices everywhere began to drift upwards once more. By the second half of 1936 the rate of inflation was quickening up, and was already high in Japan, which had enjoyed steady and rapid expansion together with full employment since early 1932. However, this revival of inflation was severely – if temporarily – moderated by the 1937 recession in the United States. Economic recovery there had been largely based on inventory accumulation and a changed climate of opinion arising from evidence of varying worth. The 1937 recession wiped out most of the gain which had occurred since March 1933: prices of farm products fell 24 per cent in the last nine months of the year, non-durables in general fell about 10 per cent in price, and wholesale prices in June 1938 were 11 per cent down on a year earlier. Recovery came with expansionary monetary measures in 1938.[60]

In Japan prices had peaked in 1920 and then fell in steps – by some 22 per cent in 1921, by 16 per cent between 1925 and 1927, by 25 per cent between 1929 and 1930, and by 15 per cent between 1930 and 1931. Prices then began to move up again, and by 1940 wholesale prices were more than double their level in 1932. Japan was by this time well integrated into the international economy, feeling the cold winds as well as the good times, but with a capacity for rapid recovery which has continued. Real wages went up in the inter-war period, yet the political and social climate then as now was not propitious for trade unions while population growth and a large agricultural sector helped to keep labour costs of industrial production down. Excessive consumption was inhibited by these circumstances, and by a regressive taxation system, which encouraged saving and capital formation by the better-off, and although her import bills were heavy during the top of the business cycle, her export growth was also substantial.

In the Soviet Union, on the other hand, things were not going so well. Between 1927 and 1937 the cost of living of the urban industrial worker seems to have risen 650 per cent while real wages declined by about 50 per cent, as money wages rose little more than three-fold. Even industrial goods prices rose by 75 per cent, in spite of the extensive use of Government subsidies to the capital goods industries. These rises were despite the price falls expected in successive Five Year Plans, and seem in fact to have been due to a massive increase in short-term credit and currency provided by the State Bank in the 1930's. For instance, the currency expanded eight-fold in the period 1929-1941. Nevertheless, there were also some significant 'real' factors at work – the hoarding of materials by managers who would otherwise have been unable to meet production targets, the indulgence in what F.S. Holzman has called 'over-full employment planning', and weaknesses in the labour market. Readily perceptible inflation, in fact, continued through the Second World War and until the currency reforms of 1947.

The Second World War

By 1940 wholesale prices in most countries were well above their 1933/34 low. Prices had risen particularly fast in Belgium, Denmark, Finland, France, Italy, Norway, Rumania, Spain and Yugoslavia – by anything between 65 and 100 percent. The rises were to be rather larger in some countries between 1940 and 1946:

Wholesale Price Rises – 1946 Levels Over 1940

Belgium	2.5 times
Bulgaria	5.4 times
Czechoslovakia	2.2 times
Finland	4.3 times
France	4.6 times
Spain	2.0 times

There were some countries where inflation was more modest – Denmark, Norway, Sweden, Switzerland, and (more surprisingly) the main Western belligerents, the U.K., U.S.A. and Germany (to 1944). On the other hand, there were countries where inflation went out of control shortly before or after the war had ended, such as Austria, Greece, Italy and – most notably – Hungary.

In the U.K. it can hardly be claimed that the war was won entirely on the basis of Keynes's ideas on this subject.[61] But neither did the rate of inflation outrun that deemed inevitable by the less 'radically-minded'.[62] Indeed the official history of the Second World War concluded that in Britain 'while there was certainly some inflation, it was confined within fairly harmless limits'.[63] The cost of living went up 32 per cent between September 1939 and June 1945 (virtually all the rise taking place in the first two years of hostilities) and weekly wage rates rose almost 50 per cent in the same period. The problem of sharply rising industrial earnings, far outstripping pay rises in the armed services, caused considerable concern especially during the first two years of the war. But a battery of controls, incentives and 'utility' schemes, combined with a tax system directed at mopping-up excess spending power served the country fairly well.

Inflation was not confined to the belligerent nations. There were interesting cases among such non-belligerents as Switzerland and Cuba.[64] But of even greater interest were the inflations in Hungary, Greece, Poland, Rumania, and China. Of these, the most fascinating was the Hungarian. All of them far outstripped the 25-fold increase in Italian prices in this period.

The Early Post-War Period

Between July 1945 and July 1946, Hungary experienced the

greatest known inflation in history. As the major article on the subject stated: 'Hungary presents a case of extreme depreciation which leaves the mark behind.'[65] When the fall of the German mark had ended, the paper mark was converted into a new mark which equalled the old at the ratio of one million depreciated marks to one gold mark. When the Hungarian pengö was replaced by the new forint on 1st August, 1946, after less than a year of monetary crisis, the ratio was 400 octillions to one forint, or 828 octillions of depreciated pengö to one 1938 pengö.[66] The extraordinary basic facts of the situation were as follows:

Hungary's Inflation 1945-1946

Date Examined		*Price Index August 26th, 1939 = 100*	*Dollar Exchange On the Black Market*
1945	July	105	1,320
	August	171	1,510
	September	379	5,400
	October	2,431	23,500
	November	12,979	108,000
	December	41,478	290,000
1946	January	72,330	795,000
	February	435,887	2,850,000
	March	1,872,913	17,750,000
	April	35,790,361	232,000,000
	May	11,267 millions	59,000 millions
	June – first 2 weeks	862,317 millions	7,600,000 millions
	– second 2 weeks	954 trillions	42,000 trillions
	July –first 2 weeks	3,066,254 trillions	22,000,000 trillions
	– second week	11,426 quintillions	481,500 quintillions
	– third week	36,018,959 quintillions	5,800,000 quintillions
	– fourth week	399,623 septillions	4,600,000 septillions

The number of notes issued also increased astronomically, but not quite in proportion:

National Bank of Hungary: Note Issue *

Date	*Pëngo Value of Notes Issued*
December 31st, 1945	765,400
January 31st, 1946	1,646,000
February 28th, 1946	5,238,000
March 31st, 1946	34,002,000
April 30th, 1946	434,304,000
May 31st, 1946	65,589,000,000
June 30th, 1946	6,277,000,000,000,000
July 31st, 1946	17,300,000,000,000,000,000

*The official source of this data implies these figures refer to the *number* rather than the value of notes issued, but a simple calculation of the number of presses which would have been required to print that many notes renders this highly improbable.

The foundation for this incredible inflation had been set during the war, with the note issue increasing from 831 million pengö in 1939 to 10.7 billion pengö in 1944. Yet, until the closing months of 1944, there was nothing very remarkable about Hungary's monetary situation. Then as early 1945 began to pass by, the situation deteriorated, for despite the virtual cessation of the note issue on the arrival of the Russian Army (the Hungarian Nazis had taken the bank-note reserves of the National Bank and the Russians only circulated enough for their own requirements), the cost of living rose 15-fold in four months. Revival of the note circulation at the end of April, 1945 had little initial impact on inflation until the following September, when the depreciation of the pengö accelerated. By the end of the year, Hungary was engulfed in an inflation of unprecedented proportions.

Various efforts were made to curb the inflation from December 1945. Private currency holdings and the number of notes in circulation were reduced by three-quarters, although the face value of bank deposits and other credits and liabilities were unchanged as were wages and salaries. For a few days there were substantial price falls, of up to 80 per cent, but then prices began their upward climb once more. Soon the inflation had reached such immense proportions that it was not only felt from day-to-day, but from hour-to-hour. Employees, as in Germany in 1923, no sooner received their pay than they rushed out to buy what they could.

In order to maintain the real value of tax yields, a new and special form of money made its appearance in January 1946 – the tax pengö. It was stipulated that tax would be payable according to the amount stipulated on the tax notice multiplied by a factor corresponding to the daily published price index. Taxpayers' liabilities were thus designated in this new money of account, and within a few days this money was to be used in business transactions. Issued at one tax pengö = one regular pengö, a premium was quickly established for the tax pengö. On February 1st, the tax pengö was worth 1.7 regular pengö; at the end of June, 7.5 billion; on July 5th, 1.2 quintillions; on July 27th, 2 octillions. But until mid-June the tax pengö had retained its value well, and it was not until news leaked out that it was to be withdrawn, without information as to its rate of conversion, that rapid depreciation set in.

On August 1st, 1946, effective stabilization measures were introduced. The regular pengö was withdrawn from circulation and redeemed at 400 octillion pengö to 1 forint. The tax pengö, which continued to circulate as an additional form of currency, was converted at the rate of 200 million pengö to 1 forint. Thus ended the greatest inflation in history.

Compared with the Hungarian inflation, early post-war experience (say to 1960) was modest elsewhere. In the U.K. prices in general rose on average by about 5 per cent per annum. In 1946/47, 1950/51, and 1955/56 they were above this figure reflecting in particular the immediate post-war rise in import prices, sterling devaluation and the Korean War, and the investment/consumer boom, respectively.

In the United States the relaxation of war-time controls was the major cause of the 53 per cent rise in wholesale prices between January 1946 and August 1948, as costs and prices readjusted themselves. Then, after a brief recession in 1948/49, there was a 22 per cent increase in wholesale prices (retail prices went up 10 per cent) during the Korean boom.[67] For the remainder of the 1950s, inflation was kept within the 5 per cent per annum range, although perhaps the most interesting feature of the period was the way in which retail prices rose 4 to 5 per cent during the end-1956 to mid-1958 recession (wholesale prices rose less rapidly).

On the Continent of Europe experience had been very variable. In Austria the cost of living more than quadrupled between 1945 and 1948, and doubled between 1948 and 1951. Between 1951 and 1960, however, prices rose at little more than 1 per cent per annum.

In Belgium the cost of living had risen 20 per cent between 1946 and 1948, but apart from a 10 per cent leap during the Korean boom remained steady until inflation got under way again in the late 1950s. Marked inflation in the cost of living occurred in Finland, where prices almost quadrupled between 1944 and 1948, and doubled again between 1948 and 1960 with rapid rises between 1948 and 1951, and between 1956 and 1960.

In France the cost of living more than doubled between 1946 and 1948, and rose a further 50 per cent between 1948 and 1951. Prices then rose more steadily until the late 1950s, so that the cost of living in 1960 was 38 per cent above the level in 1954. In West Germany the cost of living remained very stable during the 1950s, by 1960 only 11 per cent above the 1951 level (in East Germany it is claimed that the cost of living halved over the same period, which anyone observing the standard of living there towards the end of the 1950s could readily believe). The Italian cost of living had quadrupled between 1944 and 1948, but drifted upwards only slowly thereafter, and in 1960 prices were 21 per cent over their 1953 level. In The Netherlands the cost of living rose at the same rate during the 1950s as in Italy, but prices had been much more stable during the 1940s – doubling between 1939 and 1947. But in Spain, where the cost of living rose 52 per cent between 1953 and 1960, and in Yugoslavia, where it rose 43 per cent, the 1950s were much more inflationary.

In the Soviet bloc the cost of living has seemed much more stable, as one would expect where a battery of controls and avoidance of the price mechanism either circumvents or disguises inflation. In the immediate aftermath of the war, the countries of Eastern Europe had experienced massive inflation, though none on quite the Hungarian scale. In Czechoslovakia the cost of living almost doubled between 1945 and 1946, and in Poland the cost of living rose about 77-fold between the early months of 1939 and 1945, and rose a further two-thirds between 1945 and 1948. In Rumania the cost of living had more than quadrupled between 1940 and 1944, and then rose about 470-fold between 1944 and 1947. Compared with these figures the Russian cost of living changes seem most modest, trebling between 1940 and 1947 and falling by half between 1948 and 1954. They have remained steady ever since to substantiate, what has already been suggested, that such statistics from such regimes are of limited value.

In Japan, after rapid war-time and early post-war inflation, price rises were modest through the 1950s. On the other side of the Pacific, in Latin America, there has been the universally-recognized (but only partially justified) breeding ground for post-war hyperinflation, although more recent experience in Western Europe aroused fears that the disease had moved north-eastwards. During the first decade of the post-war period, the cost of living rose as follows:

Latin American Inflation, 1946-1955
Cost of Living Increase % p.a.

Chile	120
Paraguay	120
Argentina	44
Brazil	28
Peru	22
Colombia	13
Mexico	10

(It might be noted in parenthesis that the truly banana republics in this period had an exemplary record that is rarely appreciated. The annual cost of living increase in Cuba, for instance, from 1946 to 1955 was zero; in Dominican Republic 3%; in Ecuador and Venezuela 3%; in Guatemala 4% and Honduras 5%. This did not prevent social unrest or coup d'états.)

As was long ago pointed out, the reliance of these economies on one or very few commodities for export has made them highly susceptible to movements in export prices and the terms of trade.[68] To ameliorate the situation, governments have stepped in with highly inflationary monetary policies and expansionary public expenditure programmes. While it was by no means an invariable rule, there was a tendency for those countries which enjoyed the greatest improvement in the terms of trade to suffer the least inflation. However, Brazil enjoyed a substantial improvement in her terms of trade in the decade to the mid-1950s and a high rate of inflation, while the terms of trade worsened against Cuba, but internal prices fell. Nevertheless, while the terms of trade were in general deteriorating for the developing nations, especially between 1954 and 1962 and particularly for agricultural products, these conditions did put pressure on the authorities to engage in inflationary policies.[69]

Inflation in Latin America rarely had one consequence which has been marked in most inflations through the ages. Perhaps the major beneficiaries of hyperinflation in this period on this Continent were entrepreneurs. As one authority on Brazil put it: 'It is unquestionable that inflation set in operation machinery which channelled into the hands of the entrepreneurs a growing part of the mass of income which improvement in terms of trade had generated within the economy.'[70]

By the end of the 1950s, prices had increased 600 per cent in Brazil from the level in 1948, while even faster rises were recorded in Bolivia and Chile. Indeed, the Chilean situation deteriorated sharply in the mid-1950s, and the second-half of that decade was characterized by an inflation in excess of anything elsewhere in Latin America.

Inflation Since 1960

Inflation rates have tended to rise steadily since the early 1960s almost everywhere in the world, culminating in the peak rates experienced between 1973 and early 1975.

For the first few years of this period, a good deal of attention was fixed upon Latin America once more, and especially upon Brazil. Between 1958 and 1962 Brazilian inflation was running at an annual rate of 30 per cent, but it rose to 80 per cent in 1963 and to an annual rate exceeding 100 per cent in the first quarter of 1964.

This hyperinflation brought with it not only economic and political chaos, but a growing desire for a return to stability. For economic and social reasons it was concluded that this stabilization could only be achieved through a process of 'gradualism' – a term which was to find favour in U.S. circles under somewhat similar circumstances a few years later. Savings and investments had been discouraged, assets often expropriated, speculation encouraged – especially in property and foreign currency, wage rises went to the most strident and politically powerful rather than in response to productivity or skills, and tax burdens were excessive or ill-directed. The stabilization measures introduced included generalized indexation and other encouragement for all forms of saving; a formula for wage rises which incorporated allowances for previous inflation, productivity increases, and half the expected rate of inflation in the following year; miscellaneous non-wage benefits covering housing, education, etc; tax reform and inflation accounting in respect of the valuation of assets; and a 'crawling-peg' system for adjusting foreign exchange. As a result, monetary policy did not have to be accommodating to such excessive demand as previously, while Government budget expenditures were controlled and deficits eliminated.

Inflation rates gradually began to fall – to 40 per cent in 1965/66, 20 to 25 per cent in 1967/1969, and 16 per cent in 1972 and 1973. In the first half of 1974 inflation speeded up again, but price rises abated from June of that year.[71]

Although Latin American inflation was a byword through the 1950s and 1960s, and Indonesia experienced dramatic hyperinflation in 1965/1966, attention in the industrial nations turned increasingly after the early 1960s to inflation nearer home. In the United States the 'new economics' of the Kennedy Administration contained elements which, together with tax cuts enacted under President Johnson in 1964 and an accommodating monetary policy, stoked up inflationary pressures by second-half 1965. Military expenditures were also rising at this time and were not offset by tax increases or reductions in other federal government expenditures. By the end of 1965 the Federal Reserve Bank started a policy of monetary restraint, which caused an open rift with the President, and the credit crunch was clearly operating to slow demand and inflation pressures by second-half 1966. Consumer prices had risen by 3.3 per cent in the year ended December 1966, and although they rose again by 3.1 per cent in the succeeding year, wholesale prices were falling.

The situation did not improve for long. Due to Congressional inaction on a tax surcharge, and monetary relaxation by the Federal Reserve in anticipation of early Congressional action, consumer prices rose 4.7 per cent in 1968 (the wholesale price index rose 2.7 per cent and the GNP deflator by 4.1 per cent). The tax surcharge finally came into operation in June 1968, together with fairly severe fiscal constraints, which turned the federal budget round from an $11 billion deficit in first-half 1968, to a $10 billion surplus in first-half 1969. But the measures had come too late and prices were slow to respond. During 1969 consumer prices rose by 6.1 per cent, wholesale prices by 4.8 per cent, and the GNP deflator by 5.2 per cent.

With the replacement of President Johnson by President Nixon in January 1969, the 'new economists' moved out and new advisers moved in with the intention of pursuing a 'gradualist' approach to the driving down of inflation rates. Government expenditures rose, but less quickly than before; monetary growth slowed, and had ceased by the end of the year; the tax surcharge was continued, although at a reduced rate, and investment subsidies were cut. But, although the rate of growth of demand was cut right back, the impact on prices was disappointing. The implicit GNP deflator rose by 5.2 per cent during the year, and although inflation was slowing in the latter part of the year, the final quarter rise was still 4.7 per cent at an annual rate. As the economy was clearly running the risk of going into recession, and real GNP actually fell 0.6 per cent in 1970, helped down by a strike at General Motors, a policy of monetary ease combined with continued fiscal restraint was adopted. Despite the movement of real output, which was weaker than anticipated, the GNP deflator rose faster than anticipated at 5.3 per cent. Consumer price rises, which had slowed in the two middle quarters of 1970, accelerated in the fourth quarter.

By 1971 the Council of Economic Advisers was setting a target of sharp recovery from the previous year, involving an 8 per cent growth in the money supply. Despite early claims by the Federal Reserve that their target would be more modest, monetary growth spurted ahead between February and July 1971, at an annual rate of 10.8 per cent. Then the Federal Reserve compounded the expansionary effect of this policy by resisting the cyclical recovery in interest rates.

Despite these potentially inflationary steps, inflation had clearly started to come down by mid-1971 as the lagged effects of the recession and previous monetary restraint made themselves felt. However, just at this point, the President announced his Economic Stabilization Programme of 15th August, 1971: dollar devaluation (in effect); selective tax reductions; the freezing of prices and incomes for 90 days (Phase I) to be followed by further less restrictive phases. In the event, although a less restrictive Phase III was introduced, in January 1973, a freeze was reimposed in June 1973. Because of the slack in the economy and the slowing-down of the inflation rate already apparent, these measures appeared to work. Inflation fell appreciably during the operation of Phase II, but this in turn encouraged renewed relaxation on monetary policy as a result of which monetary growth rose at 8.3 per cent during 1972. By late 1972 economic growth had reached boom proportions, with real GNP rising at an annual rate of 8 per cent in fourth-quarter 1972 and first-quarter 1973. Businesses were running at or near to full capacity; order books for capital goods were full; wholesale prices had been rising rapidly, especially for agricultural goods and raw materials, since second-quarter 1972; and the effects of rising import prices were fortified by the effects of the 1971 dollar devaluation and the further devaluation in January 1973. Compounding these inflationary effects were also to be found the Great Russian Grain Robbery, the beef famine, and bad weather.

The rates of price increase were phenomenal. Wholesale food prices rose at an annual rate of 47.5 per cent, seasonally adjusted, in the first-half of 1973; and the wholesale prices of industrial commodities rose at an annual rate of 12.5 per cent, seasonally adjusted, in the same period. In the light of such rises, it was perhaps a relief that consumer prices only rose by 6¼ per cent in 1973 over the previous year. But monetary growth continued at a rapid rate long after prices and economic activity had started to take off, while the oil price rises of October 1973 and January 1974 not only had a deflationary impact through the terms of trade effect on national income, but also a modest inflationary impact (because the U.S. itself produces much, though a declining proportion, of the oil it requires). In 1974, therefore, consumer prices rose 11.4 per cent above 1973 levels (of which some 2½ per centage points were due to the oil price rise, or about half the inflationary impact oil price rises had on most West European nations). It was not until 1975, as economic activity continued to weaken until the second-quarter (real GNP had declined by 2.1 per cent in 1974, and fell a further two per cent in 1975), that price rises began to slow down. The year-on-year change was 8 per cent, but by the end of 1975 consumer price rises were running at an annual rate of just under 6 per cent.[72]

In the U.K. the early 1960s continued at the fairly low rates of inflation which had characterized the late 1950s. Although prices had risen at a compound rate of 4½ per cent per year between 1946 and 1960, most of the rise had occurred in 1946-48, 1950-52 and, on a more modest scale, in 1954-57. As a result, whereas prices had risen at a compound rate of 6¾ per cent a year between 1946 and 1952, they rose at 3¼ per cent a year between 1952 and 1960.[73]

From 1963, however, inflation began what appeared to be an inexorable upward trend. Average annual percentage changes in consumer prices, which had been 2.7 per cent in the later 1950s, rose to 3.5 per cent in the period 1960-65 and to 4.6 per cent in the period 1965-70. The outgoing Conservative Government had made a dash for growth, which became a customary pre-election tactic, providing $5\frac{1}{2}$ per cent growth and 3 per cent inflation in 1964. The incoming Labour Government managed 2.7 per cent growth and 4.8 per cent inflation the following year, together with a further round of grotesque election promises and 2.1 per cent growth, plus 4.4 per cent inflation in 1966. Nautical allusions by British Chancellors of the Exchequer had, at last since Mr Reginald Maudling's occupation of that office, meant the opposite of what any sailor might have assumed. Now, references were made to 'steady as she goes', and even the uninitiated became aware that sterling was finally headed for the rocks, as the long-delayed devaluation occurred in November 1967. Output grew that year by 1.8 per cent, prices rose by 3.1 per cent.[74]

Nothing daunted, the Labour Party Conference in September 1968 solemnly affirmed in its 'mid-term manifesto' that Britain was now seeing the revival of the British economy which had been hoped for by 1966. The manifesto went on: 'All of this is the result of firm action taken earlier to achieve industrial modernisation and reconstruction – to bring about a transformation of the debilitated economic structure we inherited into one capable of responding to, and taking advantage of, the technological revolution through which the world is living.' That was the year in which the gap between the rate of growth in output (3.1 per cent) and the inflation rate (4.0 per cent) was at its narrowest during that Labour Administration.

With an election looming up the following year and the prices and incomes policy breaking down, 1969 was the year in which the wraps really began to come off inflation. The trades union movement, led by local authority workers, were determined to test the power that full employment policies had progressively encouraged them to exert. These developments coincided with the lagged effects of monetary expansion (M3) which had gone on from early 1967 through 1968 and into the first quarter of 1969 at an annual rate of 7.4 per cent. It was hardly surprising that retail prices rose by 5.4 per cent in 1969, while output grew only by 1.7 per cent.

Yet Labour's successor as Chancellor of the Exchequer to Mr Callaghan had been Mr Roy Jenkins, who inaugurated a battery of measures which turned round the balance of payments, achieved a government budget surplus, and from second-quarter 1969 to first-quarter 1970, a very modest growth in the money supply. Almost immediately on the accession to power of a new Conservative Government in June 1970, these policies were relaxed, despite their commitment to 'stable prices'. The money stock (M3) rose at an annual rate of 8.5 per cent in the third quarter and 9.5 per cent in the fourth quarter. A budget deficit immediately opened up and increased to nearly £4.3 billion in 1973-74, which raised serious questions over the wisdom of the Government in reducing taxation (including insurance contributions) from 38 to 32 per cent of GNP between 1970 and 1973. However, it was not to be expected that a reduction in the top rate of tax on earned income from 91 to 75 per cent, or a reduction in the standard rate from 41¼ per cent (less 'earned' income relief) to 30 per cent, would be unwelcome or undesirable on other grounds.

The rate of inflation speeded up. Retail prices, which had risen 5.4 per cent the previous year, rose 6.4 per cent in 1970. The internal purchasing power of £1 had fallen 31p between 1964 and 1970, losing 8p of its value in 1970 alone (during the Conservative Administration of June 1970 to February 1974 it lost 28p of its value in all).

But there was worse to come. With economic activity slowing in 1971, and rumour of 1 million unemployed to come the following winter, the Government maintained the expansionary monetary and fiscal measures of the previous year. In no quarter during 1971 did the growth of the money stock (M3) fall below an annual rate of 10.4 per cent. Then, in the Autumn, the Government took fright and, in its famous U-turn, went back on its election pledges which eschewed prices and incomes policies. Despite a rise in real GNP of only 1.4 per cent retail prices rose 9.4 per cent. And still the money continued to grow with exceptional rapidity, M3 at an annual rate between 23.6 per cent and 28.1 per cent in each quarter between second-quarter 1972 and first-quarter 1974.

Retail prices rose further – by 7.1 per cent in 1972, and by 9.2 per cent in 1973. Wholesale prices of materials and fuels purchased by manufacturing industry rose nearly 26 per cent between second quarter 1972 and second quarter 1973; by 60 per cent in the following year; and by a further 6 per cent in the year ending second quarter 1975.

The question must be asked how much of the blame for the

monetary expansion should be laid at the door of the Bank of England's printing presses. Coins and notes in circulation plus current account deposits in banks (the M1 definition of the money supply) rose much less rapidly than the wider M3 definition, which was in turn swollen in part because of a desirable switch to more competition in banking in 1971. Thus, between the later part of 1971 and that of 1972, M1 rose $16\frac{1}{2}$ per cent, while M3 rose 26 per cent, and the following year, M1 rose less than 8 per cent, while M3 rose 28 per cent. These differences should themselves temper the weighty criticisms which have been made of the monetary authorities at this time. And in the light of the enormous rises in wholesale prices – agricultural products and industrial raw materials from early 1972, and then the oil price rises from late 1973 – either further modification of the criticism is necessary, or some clear perception of the alternatives and their impact on output and unemployment.

Prices rose a further 16 per cent in 1974 and just over 24 per cent in 1975, wage increases – particularly among strongly unionised employees – were rapid and occasionally exceeded 30 per cent a time. Administrative grade civil servants received increases of almost 100 per cent in three years while many National Health Service workers (whose numbers had grown enormously while the number of hospital beds declined) received a 70 per cent wage rise in one year.[75] Indexation schemes were introduced, and it appeared that inflation might be completely out of control. But a measure of monetary and fiscal restraint had been introduced and slack was building up in the economy (real GNP was stagnant in 1974 and fell in 1975 by some 2 per cent, after rising 5.3 per cent in 1973). Speeding up the controversial process of income redistribution which had been at work for some years, a redistributive and inflationary incomes policy was introduced from August 1975. Those earning over £8,500 per annum, many of whom had seen their real incomes fall by 20 per cent or more between mid-1970 and mid-1975, were not allowed any increase. By early 1976, their real incomes had fallen 35 per cent or more from mid-1970 levels. Yet for those of the lower paid with access to subsidized accommodation and other benefits, their discretionary income with rises up to £6 per week had never been so high. By late 1975, retail prices were running at an annual rate of under 15 per cent, and temporary euphoria about the likelihood of further sharp declines in the rate of inflation had arisen.

Nevertheless, it was hardly surprising that such massive increases in the money supply should encourage the belief that inflation during the 1967-68 and 1970-75 periods was the result of monetary laxity. An impressive volume of evidence and argument was built up to support this thesis.[6] There was a good deal of truth in it – but not the whole truth.

Unfortunately, there was a tendency for debates on inflation in the U.K. and the U.S.A. to deteriorate in the later 1960s and early 1970s into a clash between adversaries advancing single-factor explanations, while often talking at cross-purposes. The two single-factor schools were the monetarists on the one hand, and wage-push (or trade union 'monopoly') on the other. Yet, the monetary authorities did not increase the money supply of their own volition, but in response to a variety of pressures – political, budgetary, general demand by the public. Among these pressures were, for instance, the desire of politicians to maintain unemployment at a low level and to win elections, to spend taxpayers' money and to be seen to be doing things (not for them Adlai Stevenson's dictum 'Don't just do something, stand there').

In pursuing these aims, politicians and civil servants often seemed careless of the desirability of balanced budgets, hesitant to risk unpopularity by either raising taxes or cutting expenditures. They were fortified in their actions or inactions by the intellectual respectability and political attractions of Keynesian dogma as interpreted by Lord Keynes's disciples and hangers on, and by a partial reading of the 1944 White Paper on Employment. Both the politicians and the bureaucrats of central and local government had a tendency to want to expand their own sphere of influence and power, which for the bureaucrats also involved the expansion of their numbers.

Among the public more generally, the pressures of a consumer society, loathe to save and invest and in many ways actively discouraged from doing so, maintained heavy pressures on final demand, which often seemed excessive in relation to poor productivity and total output growth. Labour productivity was sometimes adversely affected by poor management, more often by the overmanning which had grown up over time and which was fortified by shop-floor conservatism and trade union attitudes. As the 1960s wore on and the 1970s came, the trade union movement in the guise of the Trades Union Congress (not always representative of its individual members at the shopfloor level) increasingly emerged as a Fourth Estate, seemingly aided and abetted by a Civil Service that nimbly shifted ground to accommodate their new masters. Government by T.U.C. White Paper, rather than by Government White Paper or even Parliamentary legislation, arrived. It was not only those on fixed incomes who lost ground, but managers in industry and commerce, skilled and highly trained people in academic life and many of the professions, many of the less well-organized and of the unemployed.

There were, in fact, three sorts of pressure increasingly at work. Cost pressures existed because of higher import prices caused by producers raising their prices and the devaluation of sterling, and because of upward pressures on labour costs. Demand pressures existed because of deficit financing, monetary and credit expansion, and the heavy demands of a consumer society wanting their jam today. Supply pressures existed because of low productivity and total output rises, and because labour disputes and bottlenecks in distribution hampered supply further.

A major change had occurred in the socio-political environment over these years. Monetary policy was permissive, but could it realistically have resisted those pressures? When, perhaps regrettably and short-sightedly, little effective opposition was mounted against such pressures, it could hardly be expected that the monetary authorities would do so. Thus, to claim without any qualification that increases in the money supply have been the cause of inflation in recent years, is neither helpful nor meaningful. The problem recently, as so often in the past, has been multi-faceted and only the natural desire of human beings to seek oversimplified explanations for highly-complex and not fully comprehensible problems, has caused the advancement of single-factor explanations.

We have a long way to go before the causes of inflation are fully understood, yet we know sufficient to be aware of those policy actions which will encourage inflation and those which will inhibit it. If we look to the recent past, we know that expansionary monetary policy has encouraged inflation, but we are neither able to isolate the effects of monetary policy entirely from fiscal policy in an era when both have been in operation, even if sometimes working in opposite directions; nor are we able to distinguish the effects of monetary policy from other inflationary pressures even when it can reasonably be argued that only a permissive monetary policy allowed these other pressures to come into full play.

These arguments spilled over into other countries, although the influence of Keynesian ideas, the conceit that policy-makers had the ability to 'fine-tune' their economies, socialist dogma, and loss of backbone among the middle classes, were often much less in evidence. In West Germany, the economic miracles of Dr Erhard in the late 1950s and early 1960s became a little tarnished with time, but consumer prices rose less quickly than in the U.S.A. or U.K. – at 2.7 per cent per annum through the 1960s. Then, with the rise of socialists to power in Germany coinciding with the intensifying pressures of inflation in the international economy, consumer prices started to rise more sharply – by 5.2 per cent in 1971, 5.6 per cent in 1972, 7.2 per cent in 1973, 7.0 per cent in 1974, and by under 6 per cent in 1975.

France fared less well on prices (though better on economic growth than West Germany and twice as well as the U.K. in the 1960s), which rose from an annual average of 3.7 per cent in the early 1960s, to 4.3 per cent in the late 1960s. Inflation continued to rise thereafter, consumer prices increasing by 5.5 per cent in 1971, 6.2 per cent in 1972, 7.3 per cent in 1973, 13.7 per cent in 1974, and by $11\frac{1}{2}$ per cent in 1975.

Other Continental European countries showed a similar tendency for prices to rise. In The Netherlands consumer prices rose 3.4 per cent a year, on average, in the early 1960s, and by 4.9 per cent in the rest of the decade. Then – as elsewhere – lift-off occurred, to 7.5 per cent in 1971, 8.5 per cent in 1972, 9 per cent in 1973, 10 per cent in 1974, and just over 10 per cent in 1975. Italy fared better on prices for many years, with inflation rising more slowly in the second half of the 1960s (2.9 per cent annual average) than in the first half (4.9 per cent annually). But prices rose just over 19 per cent in 1974, and nearly 17 per cent in 1975. Of the West European nations in 1975, only West Germany, Austria, Denmark, Sweden and Switzerland kept consumer price rises in single figures, and of those, only Germany and Switzerland managed to do so by a comfortable margin.

Yet, of all the main industrial nations, the record for persistently high inflation since 1960 must go to Japan (which, with a real GNP growth rate averaging over 11 per cent between 1959/60 and 1970/71 and rises of over 9 per cent in 1972 and almost 10 per cent in 1973, also had the best chance of coping with this). Japanese consumer prices rose on average at 6.2 per cent a year in the early 1960's, and at 5.6 per cent in the later 1960s. But it was not until 1973 that inflation climbed into double figures, at 11.8 per cent, then to nearly 24½ per cent in 1974 – a rate of increase which was halved in 1975.

By early 1976, inflation almost everywhere was slowing down although, considering the severity of the 1974/75 recession, price rises remained rapid. Whether inflation rates will continue on their downward path, or with renewed economic recovery turn up again, is one of the great imponderables of the present time. In the mid-1970s, however, it began to look as if the international economy might have reached a period when the major nations experienced cyclical fluctuations almost simultaneously, or sufficiently so as to create acute pressures on commodity supplies and industrial capacity.

Conclusions

A survey of inflation over nearly 2,500 years compressed into 20,000 words inevitably results in description at the expense of analysis. To summarize here what has already been written would be a hopeless task. But in the Appendix are charts and tables which both provide a summary and a handy reference to the major price movements of recent history.

In concluding on a note which remains descriptive rather than analytical, no apology is made. Brief analysis tends to be simplistic, and lengthy analysis often wrong. Potentially more illuminating is to close by raising a number of related issues.

Past inflations have generally been associated with rising public expenditures, the growth of bureaucracy, the increase of taxation, failing initiative and effort and faltering exports which have reflected themselves in lax monetary policies. Public expenditure in earlier times grew because of military expenditures or the costs of a standing army, more recently because of growing health, welfare and other social expenditures. Although the costs of an army have somewhat similar implications to those of a civilian bureaucracy, a civilian bureacracy may have wider ambitions: to increase the scope of its activities in order to enhance its prestige and numbers, in which it acts in concert with the ambitions of most politicians. To sustain the growing bureaucracy and its spreading commitments the burden of taxation must rise, but as the larger the burden the more it must be borne by the largest number, so the poor must increasingly feel the weight of taxation.

Professor Charles Wilson has reminded us that in the field of history one should look to the historian himself, his background and prejudices, as E.H. Carr suggested. There was a time, in the nineteenth and early twentieth centuries, when historians looking both at inflation and the decline of nations, empires and civilisations, made the burden of taxation the central point in their explanation. Whether one looked at Rome, or Spain, or The Netherlands; if one was investigating conflict in seventeenth century England or eighteenth century America. And Professor Wilson has argued that in the world of democracy and the welfare state, historians have come to accept taxation as an unavoidable and necessary adjunct of welfare, and have in consequence gone to the point where governmental actions on taxation and in related fields, tend to be overlooked as causes of inflation and economic decline.[77] Yet, we know that the burden of taxation in some advanced industrial nations has gravely inhibited the motivation, drive and willingness to take risks and accept responsibility, not only among the better-paid and highly-taxed workers, but among the lower paid as well. A major study in this area for the U.K. has drawn connections between the effects of taxation in cutting into net wage increases, industrial unrest, unemployment, declining industrial profitability, and inflation.[78]

There are tax burdens, of course, which may provide a challenge of suitable dimensions to provoke a response of greater effort. More often tax burdens have a habit of eventually exceeding the golden mean, which would provoke such a positive challenge, and have the negative effect of crushing effort and initiative.

In the meantime, and not unconnected with the increase in taxation, the bureaucracy has prospered, and being often under inadequate control, sinks into corruption or loses contact with public sentiment. To maintain its position, however, shortrun popularity is created by moderating the tax burden on politically-dangerous groups and by lax monetary policies which for a brief period give the appearance of renewed prosperity. Anyone who sustains initiative and advances themselves in the meanwhile is faced by a further extension of the tax net or prohibition on their activities, and gives up the unequal struggle. 'Envy' is fostered, as Helmut Schöek has examined in his remarkable book of that title (the post-war period in Britain may be categorized as an Age of

Envy), but failure to meet aspirations and expectations transforms the public mood into an Age of Resentment.

There is one important sense in which the general public had only themselves to blame for many of the problems that had arisen. The ambitions of politicians and bureaucrats were continually fostered by public demands that 'the Government should do this ... act now ... stop that abuse ... eradicate this problem'. Public sentiment, in reality or as conveyed in the baying of the mass media, demanded more governmental activity and public expenditure. There seemed to be a curious inability to recognize that such demands meant that the taxpayer would have to pay up, that such demands had a heavy cost. Not for nothing did public servants complain that the growth of bureaucracy was in response to public demand on the one hand, and the butt of public criticism on the other.

Occasionally, one sees it in seventeenth century Italy, eighteenth century Netherlands, and twentieth century Britain, there is a relative failure in export trade, which is a partial explanation of inflation and decline. But this explanation does not operate on its own, and most of the other socio-economic features which generally accompany inflation and economic decline have been present.

If we see recent inflation in its broader – social and political – context, therefore, the parallels multiply between Britain at the beginning of the fourth quarter of the twentieth century, and earlier empires in decline and suffering inflation. Such parallels seem, perhaps paradoxically, more persuasive though more elusive than those which see our economic and social problems in terms of long cycles, of about a quarter-century of rising prosperity followed by a quarter-century of decline. It has recently become fashionable to resurrect these Kondratieff cycles, but such notions are conceptually implausible and empirically ill-founded.[79]

Historical precedent is not encouraging either to Britain or to some other major nations. The arbitristas in Spain from 1600 accurately analysed the country's problems, but could not change the downward course on which Spain was headed. There was correct analysis before, there has been much since. We need only to look at what many eminent economists have said about inflation over many decades and were saying about its causes in the United States by 1966, or listen to the alarm bells being rung by many British economists in late 1971 which reached the proportions of professional mass hysteria by May 1972, to confirm that the analysis has been there. But not only have most politicians, bureaucrats and members of the public chosen to ignore the warnings, they have even had the temerity to charge the economists with having been caught by surprise.

There is nothing new in politicians blaming others for the difficulties they have themselves brought about or exacerbated. There is nothing new in bureaucrats maintaining and expanding their grip on political and societal institutions regardless of the part they have played in causing or exacerbating economic difficulties. It is also perfectly predictable that the public at large should seek scapegoats for economic problems when the true culprits are partially hidden and deflect criticism elsewhere. But it is only when those with power – trade unionists, politicians and civil servants – get hurt by inflation and can no longer successfully demand privileged treatment to avoid its consequences, that the control of inflation will seriously be attempted. At the present juncture, in Britain at least, demands for privileged treatment by the main power groups outweigh demands that the underlying causes of inflation be serious tackled.

Notes

1. J. Boardman: 'The Greeks Overseas', 1964. p. 79. Harmondsworth.
2. M. Rostovtzeff: 'The Social & Economic History of the Hellenistic World', 1941. p. 96. Oxford. Since the above was written a popular study drawing many parallels between the fall of the Roman Empire and recent times has appeared, Michael Grant: 'The Fall of the Roman Empire – A Reappraisal', 1976. Annenberg School Press.
3. M. Rostovtzeff: 'The Social & Economic History of the Roman Empire', 1926. p. 419. Oxford.
4. R. Duncan-Jones: 'The Economy of the Roman Empire: Quantitative Studies', 1974. pp. 7-8, 66, and 366-368.
5. Rostovtzeff, infra. p. 429.
6. A.H.M. Jones: 'The Ancient Empires and the Economy', 1969. p. 97. Paris/The Hague.
7. M.I. Finley: 'The Ancient Economy', 1973. p. 161, London.
8. Finley, supra. p. 90.
9. Rostovtzeff, infra. p. 475.
10. This coin weighed 22 grains at the end of Offa's reign; under Alfred's immediate successors its weight rose to 27 grains; until the fourteenth century the weight does not seem to have fallen below 22½ grains, but

thereafter the decline was rapid until in the early Tudor period it weighed barely 12 grains. It was also in Offa's reign (774 A.D.) that Arab coins circulating in Europe were imitated in England.

11. Georges Duby: 'The Early Growth of the European Economy'. 1974. p. 61 ff. London.
12. George Duby: 'Rural Economy and Country Life in the Mediaeval West', 1968. p. 135. London.
13. Professor Hilton has recently claimed: 'As new evidence turns up, it seems to justify rather than to contradict the view put forward here that rural social relationships in the middle ages were characterised by conflict rather than harmony of lord and peasant interests.' (R. Hilton: 'Bond Men Made Free', 1973. p. 234, London). Parallels have been drawn not only with more modern times, but also with the Roman period. Jules Toutain in 'The Economic Life of the Ancient World', 1930 remarked that 'the rise of the Bagaudae in Gaul was a perfect Jacquerie (see below) which went on for years'. (p. 325).
14. This, however, also reflected the taking into direct management of estates on an increasing scale from the late twelfth century simply because leasehold rents were so low. The thirteenth century has been described as 'the great age of economic enterprise on large estates', but there was a return to indirect management in the mid-fourteenth century. E. Miller: 'England in the Twelfth and Thirteenth Centuries: An Economic Contrast', Economic History Review, February, 1971. See also further comments by C.G. Reed, T.L. Anderson, and E. Miller in the February, 1973 issue of the Review.
15. It should not need stating nowadays that Parliament persistently complained that the Statute of Labourers was not being kept, employers frequently evading the Statute in an effort to keep their labour force, while labourers moved from place to place. There is an interesting discussion on this point in J.E. Thorold Rogers: 'Six Centuries of Work and Wages', 1901 Edition. p. 229 ff. However, once price rises could no longer keep step with wages – as they had done between 1351 and 1376 – then pressures to enforce the Statute increased.
16. Professor Mollat and Wolff have recently written: 'Among all the causes of rebellion, the instability of the monetary system and the disparity between prices and wages, acted deeply but often in a way which contemporaries failed to perceive.' M. Mollat & P. Wolff: 'The Popular Revolutions of the Late Middle Ages', 1973. p. 93. London.
17. A.R. Bridbury: 'The Black Death', Economic History Review, November 1973. p. 578. The first three decades of the fourteenth century are dealt with in M. Mate: 'High Prices in Early Fourteenth-Century England: Causes and Consequences', Economic History Review, February, 1975.
18. Fernand Braudel: 'Capitalism and Material Life, 1400-1800', 1973. p. 328. London.
19. Georg Wiebe: 'Zur Geschichte der Preisrevolution des 16. und 17. Jahrhunderts', 1895. Leipzig.
20. E.H. Phelps Brown and S.V. Hopkins: 'Seven Centuries of the Prices of Consumables, Compared with Builders' Wage Rates', Economica, November, 1956, Appendix B.
21. Curiously, very few people have noted the modest extent of inflation in the sixteenth century compared with recent times, or how it compares with

inflation in the thirteenth and early fourteenth centuries (due to bad harvests in 1316/1317 food prices doubled on five years previously), or the much more severe inflation of the third century. Notable exceptions are Professor Peter Mathias in the preface to P.H. Ramsey: 'The Price Revolution in Sixteenth Century England', 1971; and J.D. Gould in 'The Price Revolution Reconsidered', Economic History Review, Vol. XVII (1964-65).

22. Earl J. Hamilton: 'American Treasure and Andalusian Prices, 1503-1660', Journal of Economic and Business History, November, 1928.
23. The point has been stressed by F. Simiand: 'Recherches anciennes et nouvelles sur le mouvement general des prix du XVle au XIXe siecle', 1932. Paris. And by I. Hammarstrom 'The Price Revolution of the Sixteenth Century: Some Swedish Evidence', The Scandinavian Economic History Review, Vol V 1957.
24. There is no way of judging whether the influence of later marriages and smaller families, as stressed by Dr Brenner, was more significant than the impact of influenza, a thesis stressed by Professor F.B. Fisher.
25. By Professor Geoffrey Maynard in 'Economic Development and the Price Level' 1962. London.
26. J.D. Gould: 'The Price Revolution Reconsidered', Economic History Review, Vol XVII 1964-65.
27. C.E. Challis: 'The Circulating Medium and the Movement of Prices in Mid-Tudor England', in P.H. Ramsey (Ed.): 'The Price Revolution in Sixteenth-Century England', 1971. London.
28. Stressed by J.U. Nef: 'Silver production in Central Europe,' Journal of Political Economy, Vol. XLIX, 1941. pp. 584-6. Also his contribution to the 'Cambridge Economic History', Vol II.
29. Y.S. Brenner: 'The Inflation of Prices in Early Sixteenth-Century England', Economic History Review, Vol XIV, 1961-62.
30. Fernand Braudel: 'The Mediterranean and the Mediterranean World in the Age of Philip II', 1975. Vol I, pp. 326/327. London. (First published in French in 1949).
31. Earl J. Hamilton: 'American Treasure and Andalusian Prices, 1503-1660: A Study in the Spanish Price Revolution', Journal of Economic and Business History, November, 1928.
32. Earl J. Hamilton: 'The Decline of Spain', Economic History Review, May 1938. p. 169.
33. This story is told in greater detail in J.C. Vives: 'The Decline of Spain in the Seventeenth Century', first published in 'An Economic History of Spain', 1969. Chapters 29, 30. Princeton. Reprinted in Carlo M. Cipolla: 'The Economic Decline of Empires', 1970. pp. 121-167. London.
34. Carlo M. Cipolla: 'Le avventure della lira', 1958. pp. 63-4. Milan. Also the same author's 'The Economic Decline of Italy' in his 'The Economic Decline of Empires' (supra), p. 211.
35. Useful sources of reference are: T.S. Ashton: 'Economic Fluctuations in England, 1700-1800', 1959. pp. 106 ff. Oxford. Sir John Clapham: 'The Bank of England'. A.E. Feavearyear: 'The Pound Sterling', 2nd Ed. revised by Professor E. Victor Morgan. 1963. pp. 153 ff. Oxford.
36. P. Deane & W.A. Cole: 'British Economic Growth, 1688-1959', 1967. p. 17. Cambridge.
37. E.W. Gilboy: 'Wages in Eighteenth Century England', 1934. p. 220.

Harvard. M.W. Flinn: 'Trends in Real Wages, 1750-1850', Economic History Review, August, 1974.

38. A.D. White: 'Fiat Money Inflation in France', 1959. New York. First read in 1876, and first privately published in 1912, it is now available from The Foundation for Economic Education, Irvington-on-Hudson.
39. The story has been recently retold by J.K. Galbraith: 'Money: Whence It Came, Where It Went', 1975. pp. 22-27. London.
40. A manufacturer of hardware retired from business in 1790 with 321,000 livres found his property worth only 14,000 francs in 1796.
41. A.E. Feavearyear: 'The Pound Sterling', 2nd Ed. Revised by E.V. Morgan. 1963. pp. 177-201.
42. English observers were commenting on the heavy burdens of Dutch taxation, their multiple imposition on food, and their inflationary impact on labour costs and prices from the 1650s. Taxation was sufficiently heavy by 1690 for William Carr in 'An Accurate Description' (1691) to claim that if such taxes were levied in England 'there would be rebellion upon rebellion'. Professor Charles Wilson has extended this theme as a major cause of the Dutch decline in 'Taxation and the decline of empires, an unfashionable theme', Bejdragen tot de Taal-land-en Volkenkunde van Nederlandsch Indie, Vol. 77, 1963. pp. 10-26. Utrecht. Reprinted in C. Wilson: 'Economic History and the Historian: Collected Essays', 1969. pp. 114.ff. London.
43. C.R. Boxer: 'The Dutch Seaborne Empire, 1600-1800', 1965. pp. 285 and 293.
44. B.R. Mitchell: 'European Historical Statistics, 1750-1970', 1975. p. 736. London.
45. Peter Mathias in A.J. Taylor (Ed.): 'The Standard of Living in Britain in the Industrial Revolution', 1975. p. viii. London.
46. Not only were these regional disparities significant in the first-half of the century, but they persisted. A recent study has found 'regional analysis of the labour market is a powerful antidote to overdoses of pessimism concerning the effect of industrialization on living standards ...' E.H. Hunt: 'Regional Wage Variations in Britain, 1850-1914', 1973. p. 356. Oxford.
47. For the literary tradition, Michael Jefferson: 'Industrialisation and Poverty: In Fact and Fiction' in N. Gash (Int.): 'The Long Debate On Poverty', 2nd Ed., 1974. pp. 189-238. Institute of Economic Affairs, London. And Michael Jefferson: 'The Concern With Inequality in Victorian Fiction', in Aubrey Jones (Ed.): 'Economics and Equality', 1976. pp. 30-46. Philip Allan, Oxford.
48. J.H. Clapham: 'An Economic History of Modern Britain: Free Trade and Steel, 1850-1886', 1932. pp. 338-339. Cambridge.
49. S.B. Saul: 'The Myth of the Great Depression, 1873-1896', 1969. London.
50. P. Deane & W.A. Cole: 'British Economic Growth, 1688-1959', 1967: p. 18. Cambridge.
51. K. Ohkawa: 'The Growth Rate of the Japanese Economy since 1878', 1957. Tokyo.
52. Milton Friedman and A.J. Schwartz: 'A Monetary History of the United States, 1867-1960', 1963. pp. 115-138. Princeton.
53. E. Victor Morgan: 'Studies in British Financial Policy, 1914-1925', 1952. pp. 73-74 and 80-81. London.
54. The stand taken by Professor A.S. Milward in 'The Economic Effects of the

Two World Wars in Britain', 1970. p. 28. London.

55. William Guttmann and Patricia Meehan: 'The Great Inflation: Germany, 1919-1923', 1975. p. 61. Saxon House, Hampshire.
56. Excerpts from Pearl S. Buck (p.120-146) and from leading German figures during the Great Inflation, such as Rudolf Havenstein and Hugo Stinnes, are most conveniently to be found in F.K. Ringer (ed.): 'The German Inflation of 1923', 1969, Oxford.
57. Erich Kästner: 'Fabian', trans. by Cyrus Brooks, 1932, London.
58. Adam Fergusson: 'When Money Dies: The Nightmare of the Weimar Collapse', 1975, p. 226, London.
59. The classic statement on 'the great contraction' is in Milton Friedman and Anna Jacobson Schwartz: 'A Monetary History of the United States, 1867-1960', 1963, pp. 299-419, Princeton. However, their work over-emphasises the monetary explanation whereas a more recent work by J. Potter: 'The American Economy between the World Wars', 1974 (London) goes to the other extreme in emphasising other hypotheses.
60. Charles P. Kindleberger: 'The World in Depression, 1929-1939', 1973, pp. 262-277, London.
61. John Maynard Keynes: 'How to Pay for the War: A Radical Plan for the Chancellor of the Exchequer', 1940, London.
62. Lionel Robbins was 'inclined to believe that the technical reasons I have adduced make it extremely improbable that some degree of inflation can be avoided'. 'The Economic Problem in Peace and War', 1957, p.36, London. One is tempted to add that the same point could have been made without engaging in technicalities.
63. W.K. Hancock and M.M. Gowing: 'British War Economy', 1949, p. 343, London.
64. Leland B. Yeager: 'International Monetary Relations: Theory, History, and Policy', 1966, pp. 335-339, New York.
65. Bertrand Nogaro: 'Hungary's Recent Monetary Crisis And Its Theoretical Meaning', American Economic Review, September, 1948, p. 526.
66. One Octillion = 10^{27}
    One Septillion = 10^{24}
    One Quintillion = 10^{18}
67. It should be pointed out that wholesale price indices do not always indicate transactions prices, but may only indicate the much less volatile list prices. This is one of the traps into which some researchers into the thesis that large firms 'administer' prices have fallen. The major study in this area, which investigates U.S. prices, is G.J. Stigler and J.K. Kindahl: 'The Behaviour of Industrial Prices', 1970, New York.
68. Geoffrey Maynard: 'Economic Development and the Price Level', 1962, pp. 242-275, London.
69. In the half-century before the Second World War there had been, on the other hand, a much larger improvement in the terms of trade than this post-war deterioration. But the rate of deterioration varied between product groups, and was – 32 per cent for the coffee, tea and cocoa group between 1950/54 and 1961/65. Paul Bairoch: 'The Economic Development of the Third World Since 1900', 1975, pp. 126-134, and 199, London.
70. Celso Furtado: 'The Economic Growth of Brazil', 1963, pp. 248-249, California.

71. Roberto de Oliveira Campos: 'Inflation in Brazil – The Principles of Monetary Correction', Chairman's Lecture, London Stock Exchange, 19th November, 1974. Campos, as Minister of Finance, was the main architect of Brazil's stabilisation programme. Also, Alexandre Kafka in 'Essays on Inflation and Indexation', American Enterprise Institute, Washington. October, 1974.
72. One of the most useful books on the 'new economics' is Herbert Stein: 'The Fiscal Revolution in America', 1969, Chicago. The Annual Reports of the Council of Economic Advisers are useful as reflecting official opinion, and the Brookings Papers on Economic Activity are occasionally excellent. Unrivalled for the more recent period are selected publications of the American Enterprise Institute, Washington, D.C.: Phillip Cagan: 'Recent Monetary Policy and the Inflation', 1971. Marten Estey: 'Wages, Wage Policy and Inflation, 1962-1971', 1971. Gottfried Harberler: 'Incomes Policies and Inflation', 1971. T.G. Moore: 'U.S. Incomes Policy, Its Rationale and Development', 1971. Phillip Cagan et al: 'Policy and Inflation in the Sixties', 1972. Phillip Cagan: 'The Hydra-Headed Monster: The Problem of Inflation in the United States', 1974.
73. J.C.R. Dow: 'The Management of the British Economy, 1945-60', 1964. pp. 343-363. Cambridge.
74. Wilfred Beckenman (Ed.): 'The Labour Government's Economic Record: 1964-1970', 1972 p. 298. London. Mr Samuel Brittan's 'Steering the Economy', 1971. (Harmondsworth) is excellent on this period.
75. In a series of articles in 'The Sunday Times' (November 2, 9, 16, 1975) Robert Bacon and Walter Eltis highlighted the growth of 'non-marketed' (principally public sector) employment in the U.K. economy in recent years, and the income rises this group had obtained while remaining largely parasitical on British industry and commerce. Since the above was written their 'Britain's Economic Problem: Too Few Producers' has been published by Macmillan.
76. For example, publications by the Institute of Economic Affairs:
    A.A. Walters: 'Money in Boom and Slump', 1970.
    Milton Friedman: 'The Counter-Revolution in Monetary Theory', 1970.
    Gottfried Harberler et al: 'Inflation and the Unions', 1972.
    Lord Robbins et al: 'Inflation: Economy and Society', 1972.
    Lord Robbins et al: 'Inflation: Causes, Consequences, Cures', 1974.

    Also, important contributions in books and mimeographed papers (for the Manchester University Social Science Research Council programme on Inflation: Its Causes, Consequences and Cures), by Professors D.E.W. Laidler and Michael Parkin – both of whom have now regrettably fled the country.
77. Charles Wilson: 'Taxation and the Decline of Empires, an Unfashionable Theme', in 'Economic History and the Historian: Collected Essays', 1969, pp. 114-116. London.
78. D. Jackson, H.A. Turner and F. Wilkinson: 'Do Trade Unions Cause Inflation?', 1972. p. 102. Cambridge. Messrs. Bacon and Eltis in a series of articles in 'The Sunday Times' (November 1975) have also mentioned this factor.
79. Nikolai D. Kondratieff's thesis is most conveniently found in: 'The Long Waves in Economic Life', Review of Economic Statistics, November, 1935

(p. 105-115). This article is reprinted in American Economic Association: 'Readings in Business Cycle Theory', 1944 (pp. 20-42). The best critique of Kondratieff is by George Garvy: 'Kondratieff's Theory of Long Cycles', Review of Economic Statistics, November 1943, (pp. 203-220). Kondratieff claimed to have found:
First long wave:
(i) Rise from late 1780s or early 1790s to 1810-1817.
(ii) Decline from 1810-17 to 1844-51.
Second long wave:
(i) Rise from 1844-51 to 1870-75.
(ii) Decline from 1870-75 to 1890-96.
Third long wave:
(i) Rise from 1890-96 to 1914-20.
(ii) Decline from 1914-20.

The theory has its superficial attractions, of course, and price movements, as we have seen, come nearer than the physical series Kondratieff also presented in supporting his views. A superficial attempt was made in 1972 to apply Kondratieff's work to the future of the United States by James B. Shuman & David Rosenau: 'The Kondratieff Wave: The Future of America Until 1984 and Beyond', 1972. Delta Publishing, New York.

APPENDIX

It cannot be overstressed that there are always defects in price series, which make precise statements about changes in price levels over time of dubious value. These defects are compounded when, as occurs in a number of the following charts, different or even very similar indices are linked together. The results should therefore be taken as indicating the broad movement of prices in the various countries concerned and the data in this wider context are sufficiently reliable for that.

Nevertheless, the movement in prices tells us little about changes in standards of living or real incomes and, when we are considering wholesale price movements, may not tell us much about the cost of living. To these problems are added, by Charts 1 and 2, the difficulty in judging the components and weights of a basket of consumer goods when product availability, tastes and standard of living change over time.

CHART 1

U.K. PRICES OF A COMPOSITE UNIT OF CONSUMABLES – A.D. 1260 to 1620 (AFTER PHELPS BROWN AND HOPKINS)

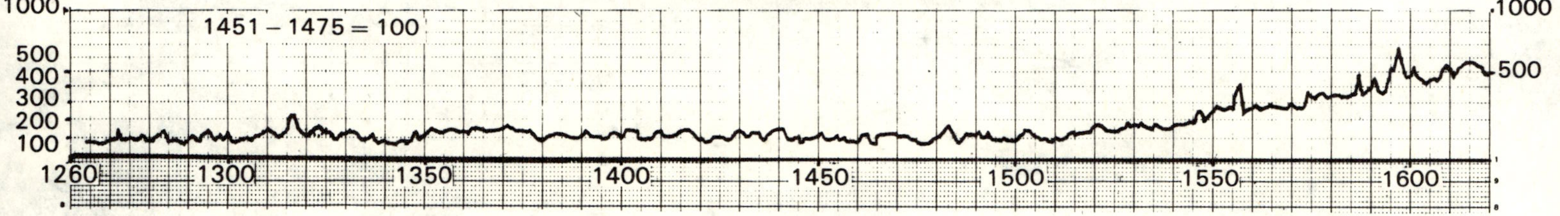

CHART 2

U.K. PRICES OF A COMPOSITE UNIT OF CONSUMABLES – A.D. 1600-1960 (1976) (AFTER PHELPS BROWN AND HOPKINS)

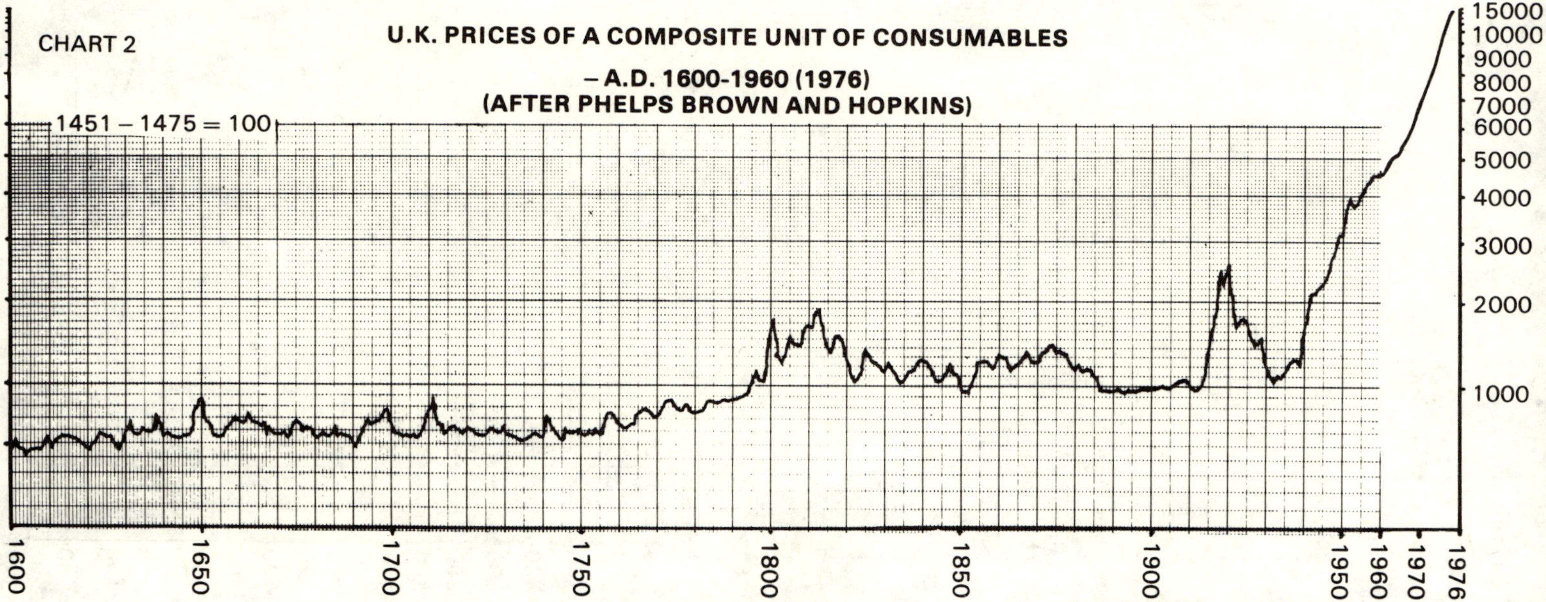

CHART 3

U.K. PRICES 1660-1910

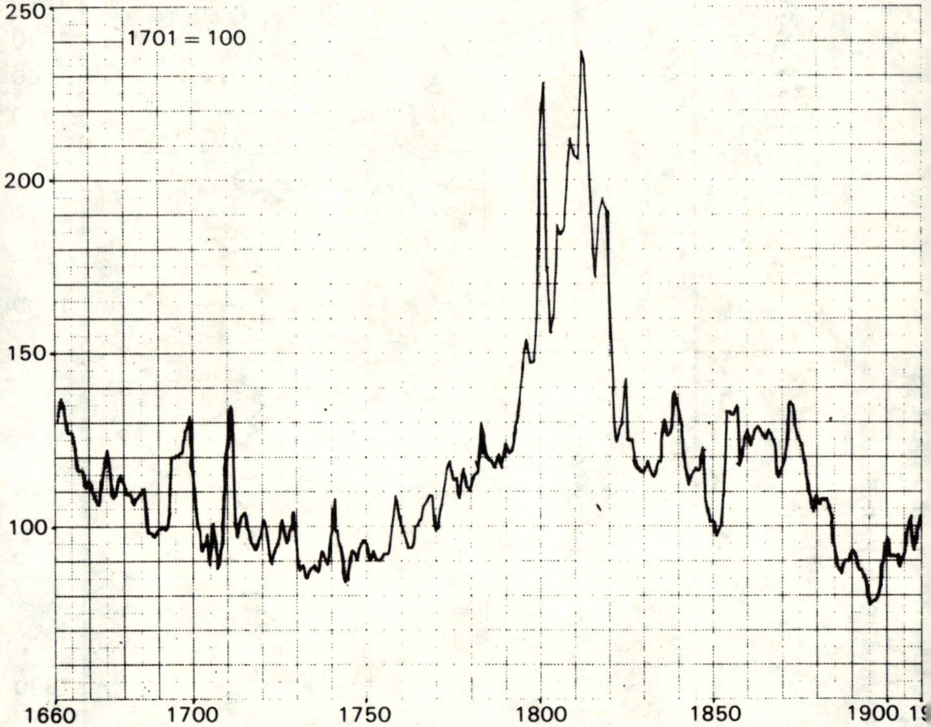

CHART 4

U.K. – BOARD OF TRADE WHOLESALE PRICES
1871-1948

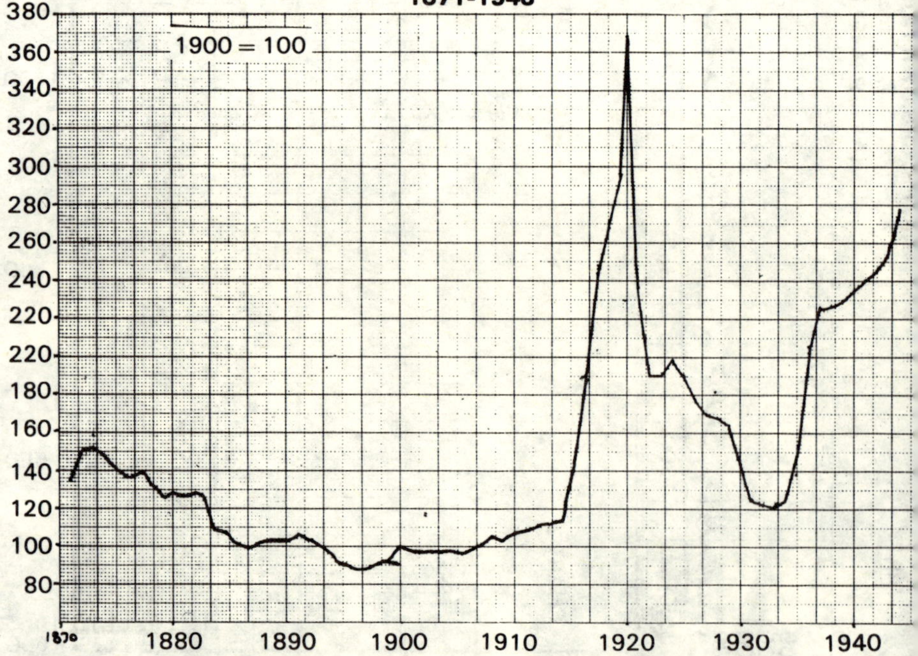

CHART 5

U.K. RETAIL PRICES 1900-1963

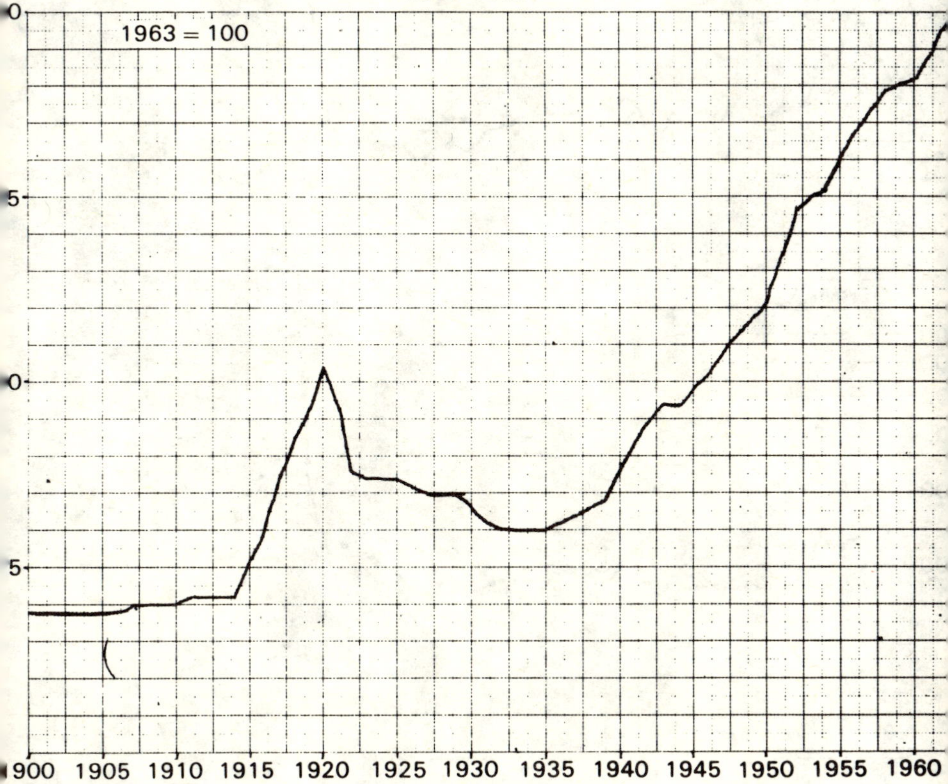

CHARTS 6 **WHOLESALE PRICES IN FRANCE AND GERMANY 1800 to the mid 1940s; AND IN SPAIN, 1812 to the mid 1940s.**

1913 = 10

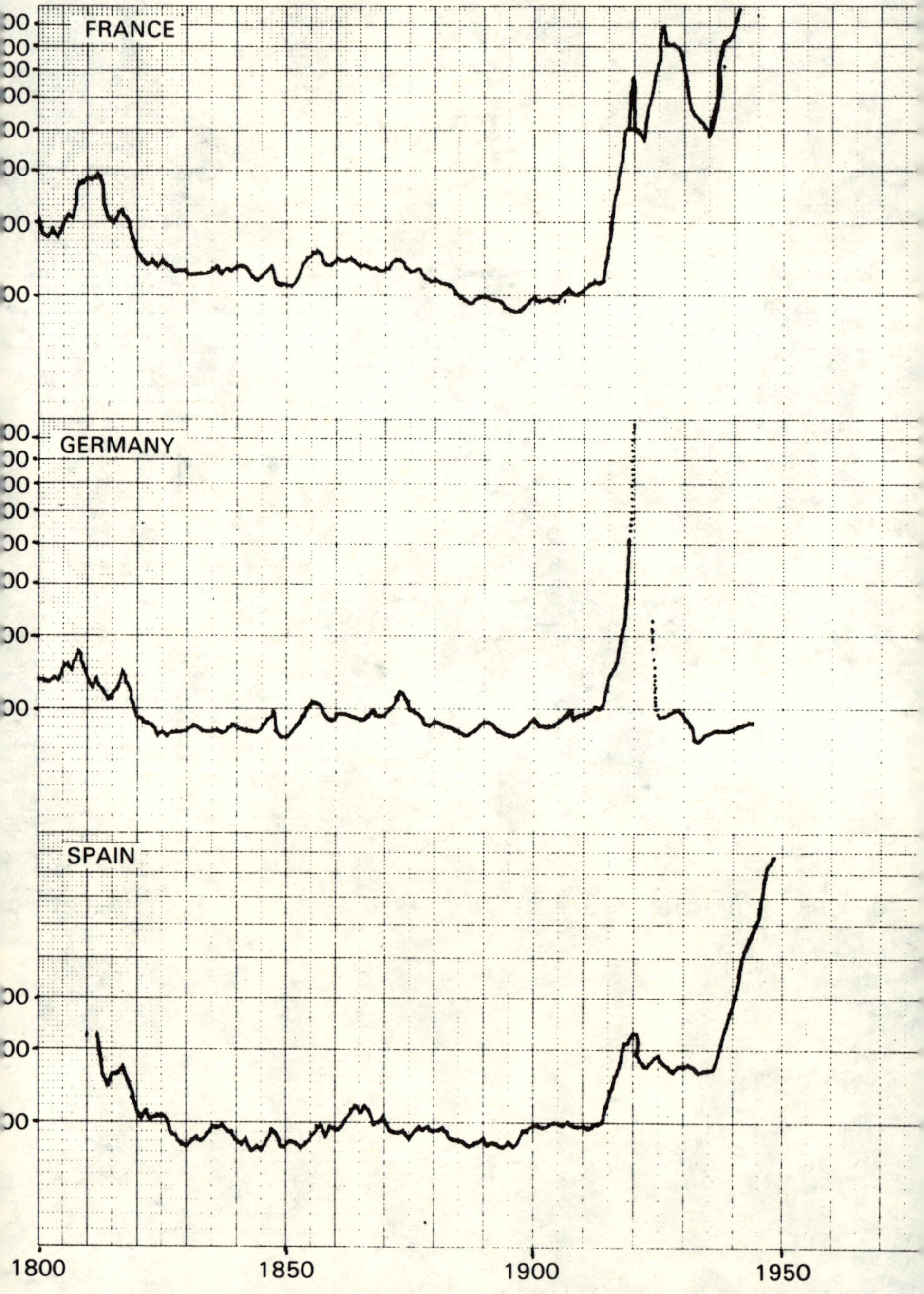

CHARTS 7 **WHOLESALE PRICES IN BELGIUM, ITALY AND SWEDEN, 1860-1940 (approx.)**

1913 = 100

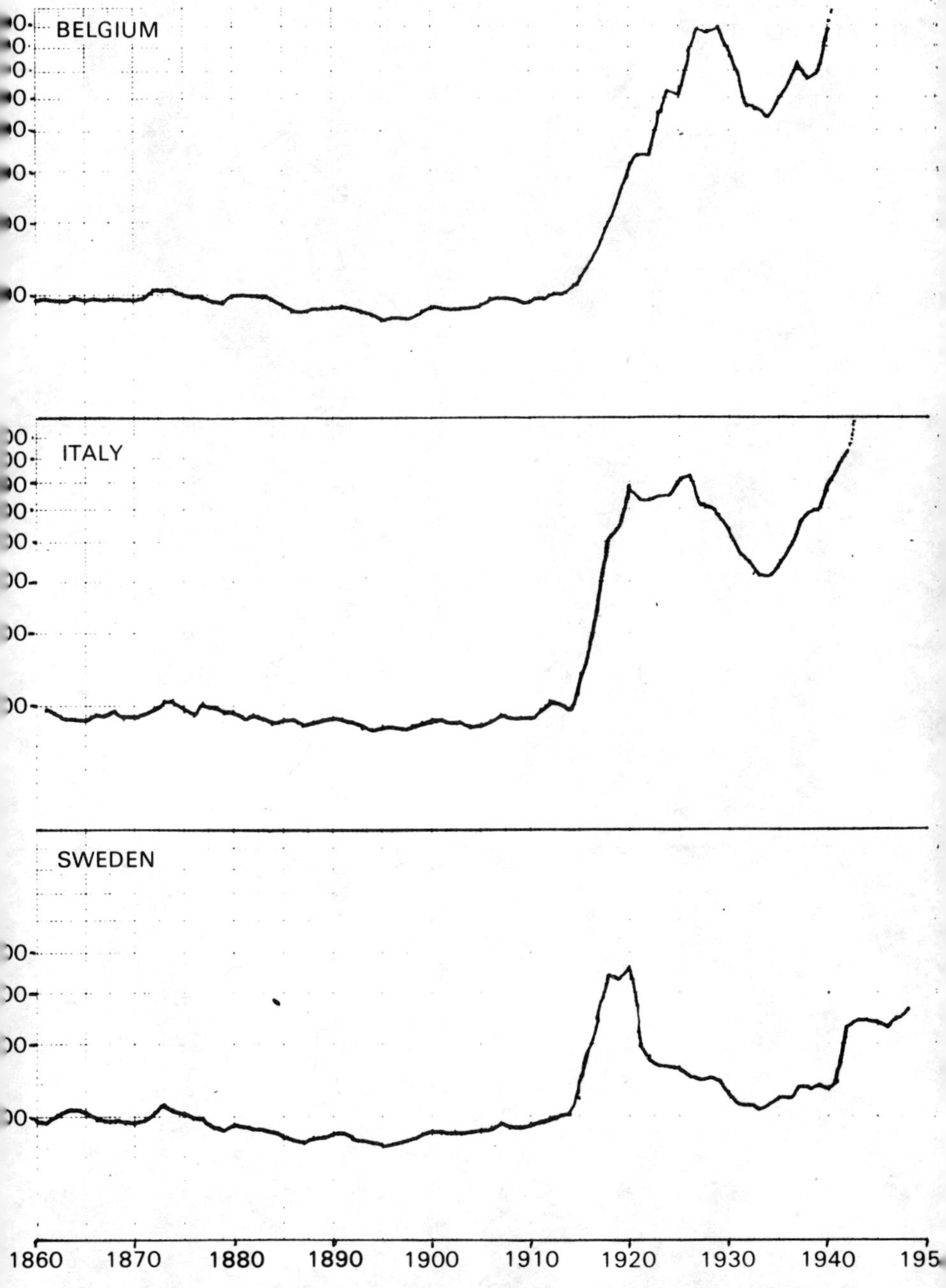

CHARTS 8

WHOLESALE PRICES IN THE NETHERLANDS AND NORWAY, 1900-1948 AUSTRIA 1922-1948

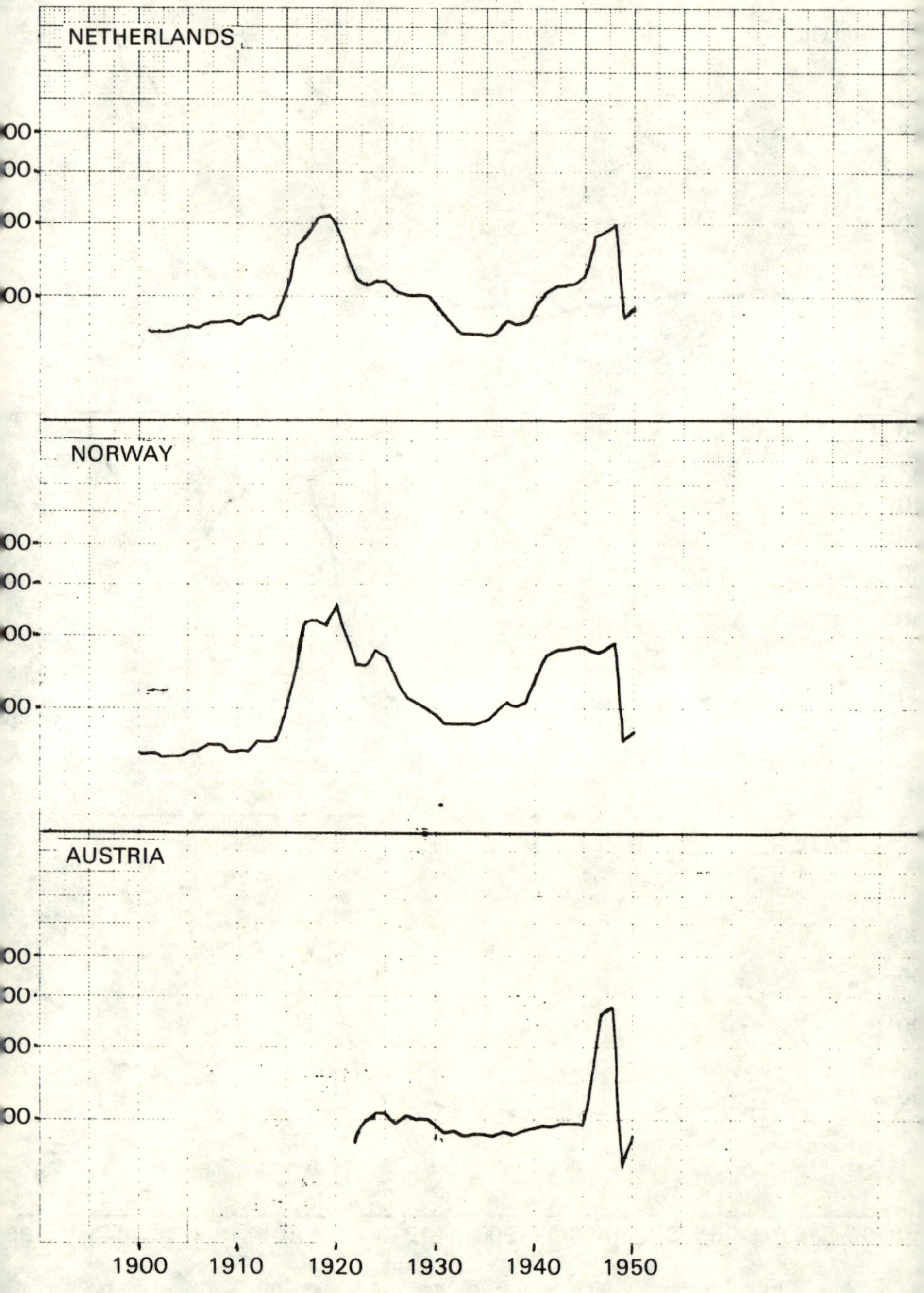

CHARTS 9

COST OF LIVING IN BELGIUM, FRANCE AND GERMANY 1840-1900

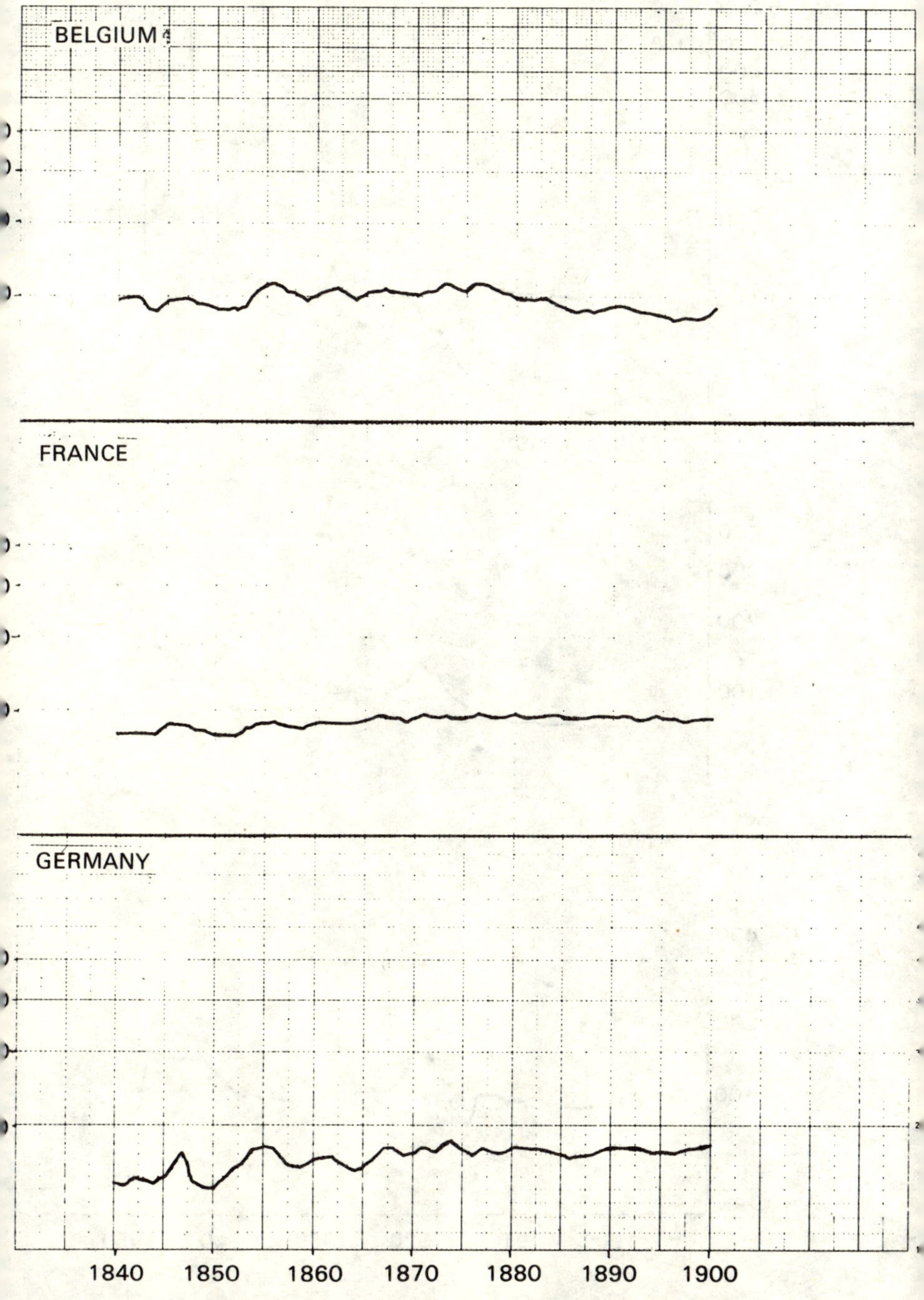

CHARTS 10

COST OF LIVING IN ITALY THE NETHERLANDS AND SWEDEN, 1900-1950

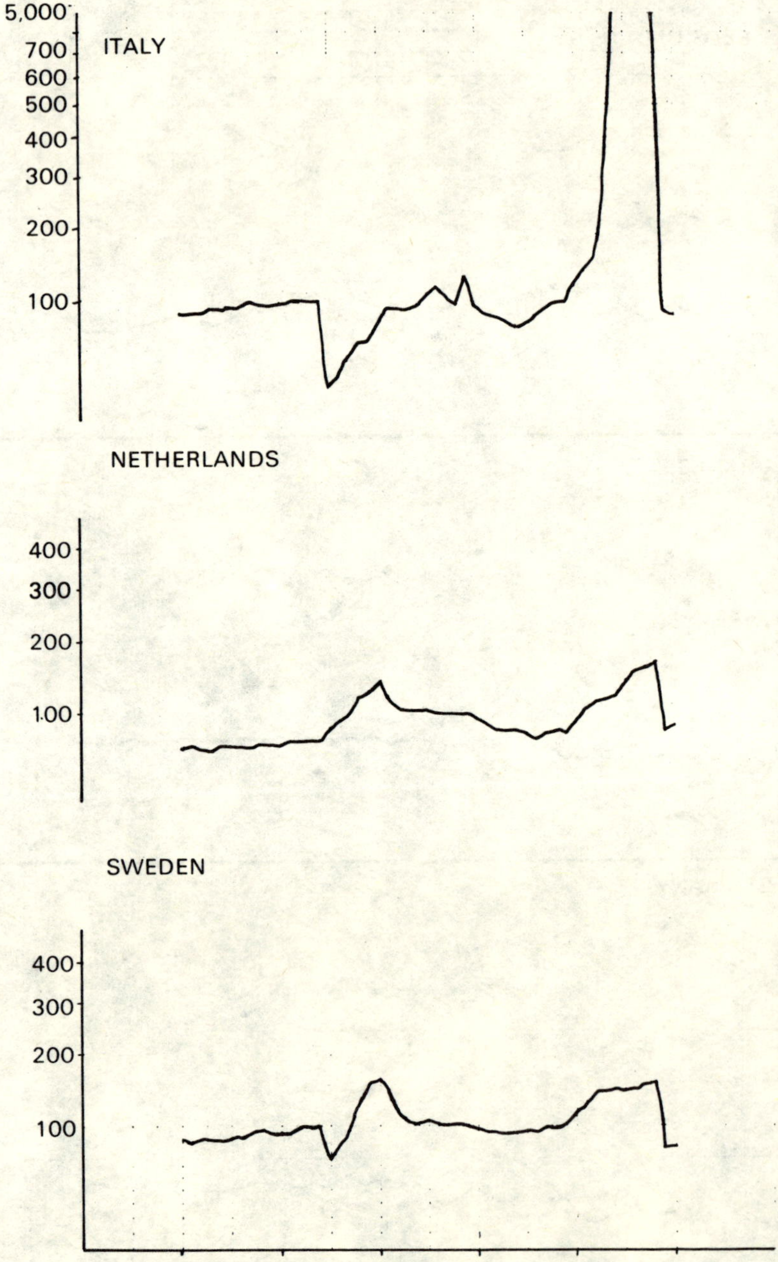

CHART 11

U.S. WHOLESALE PRICE INDEX
1749-1957
(1910/1914 = 100)

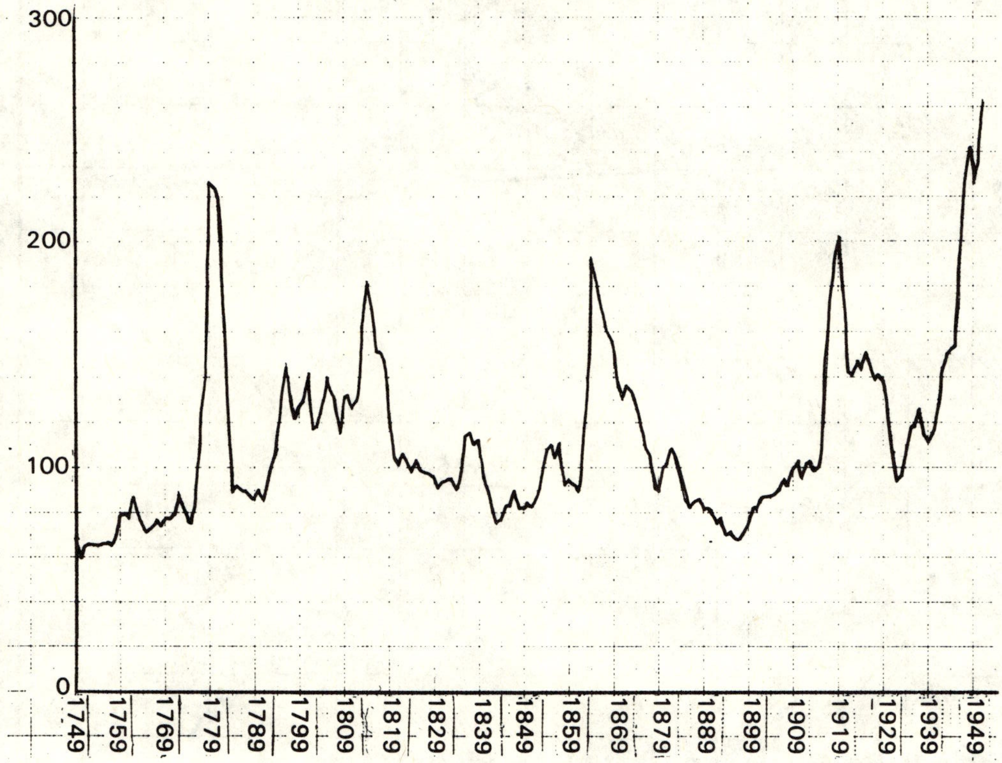

CHART 12

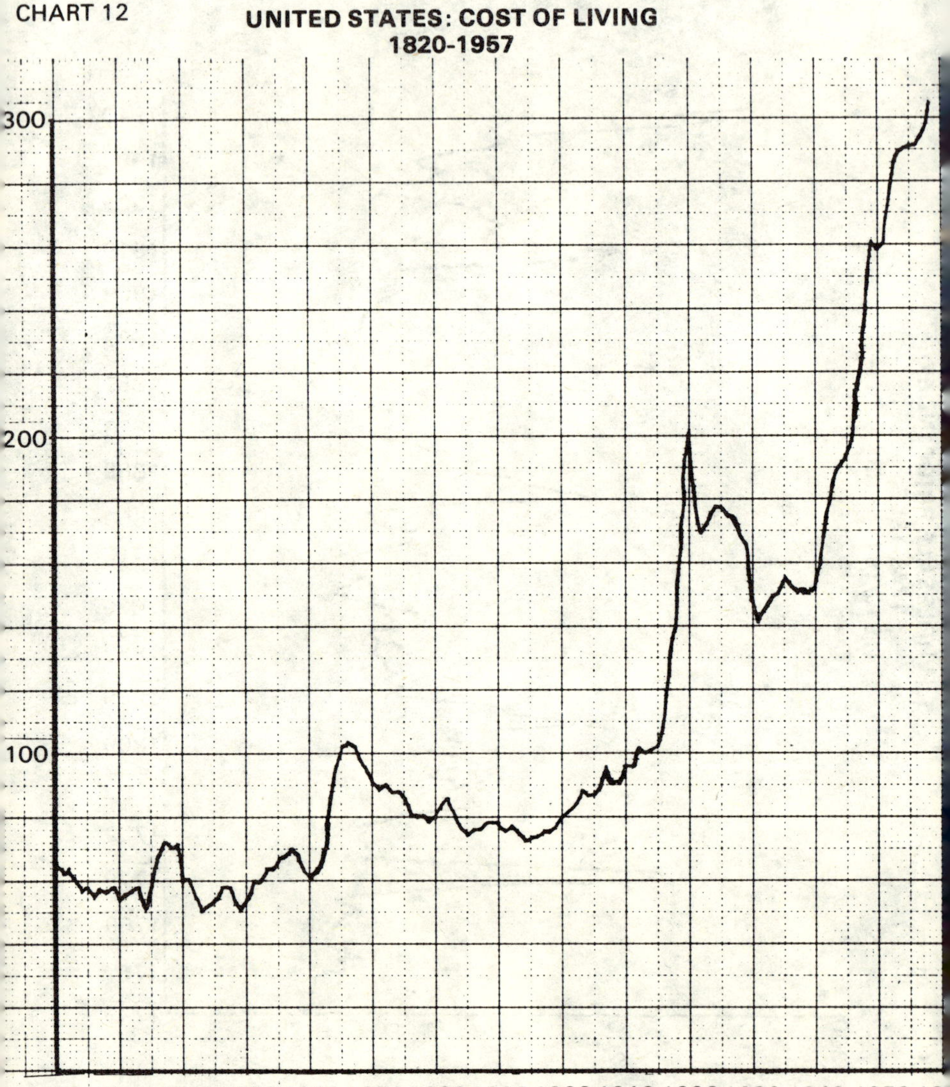
UNITED STATES: COST OF LIVING
1820-1957
300
200
100
1820
1830
1840
1850
1860
1870
1880
1890
1900
1910
1920
1930
1940
1950
19

CHART 13(a)

USA: PRICE INDICES OF PRIVATE CONSUMPTION, CHANGES (1950-1975)

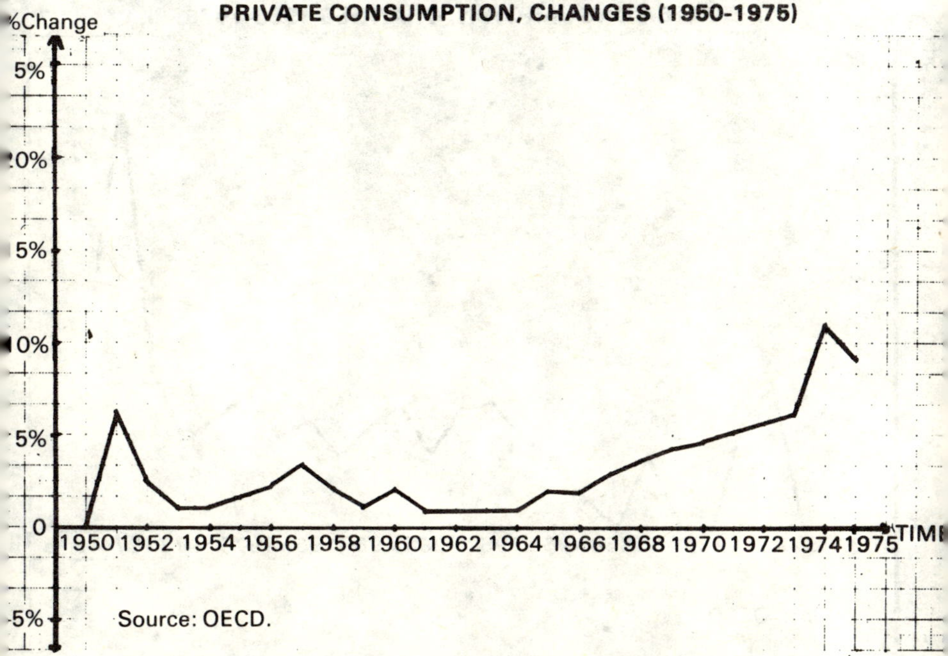

CHART 13(b)

U.K.: PRICE INDICES OF PRIVATE CONSUMPTION, CHANGES 1950-1975

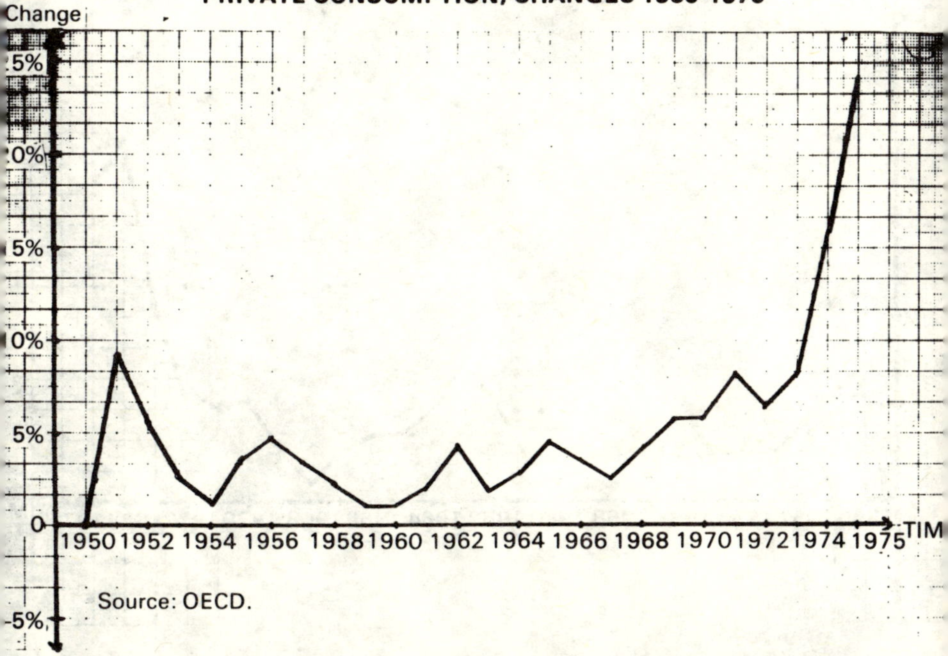

CHART 13(c)

JAPAN: PRICE INDICES OF PRIVATE CONSUMPTION, CHANGES 1950-1975

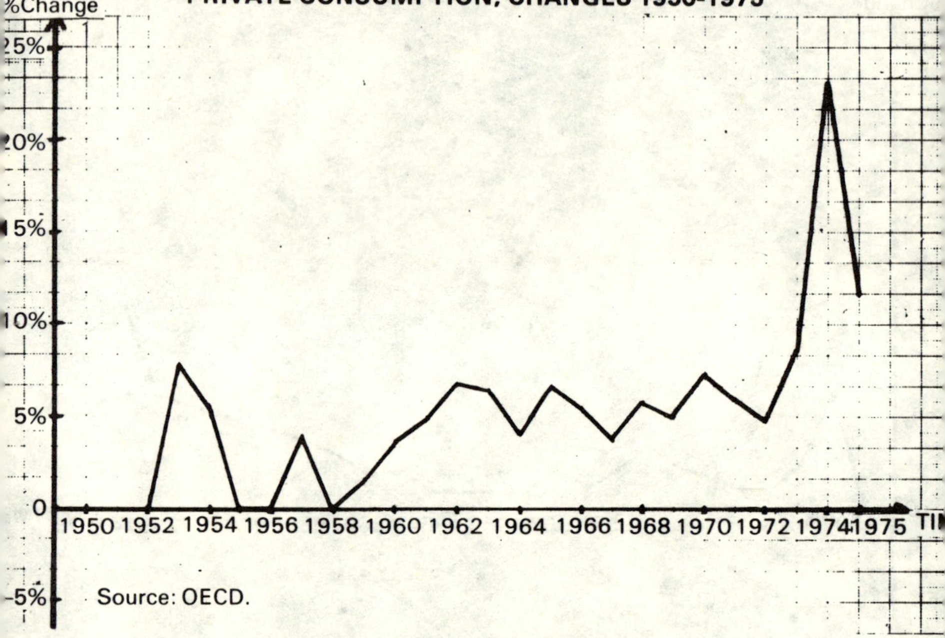

Source: OECD.

CHART 13(d)

ITALY: PRICE INDICES OF PRIVATE CONSUMPTION, CHANGES 1950-1975

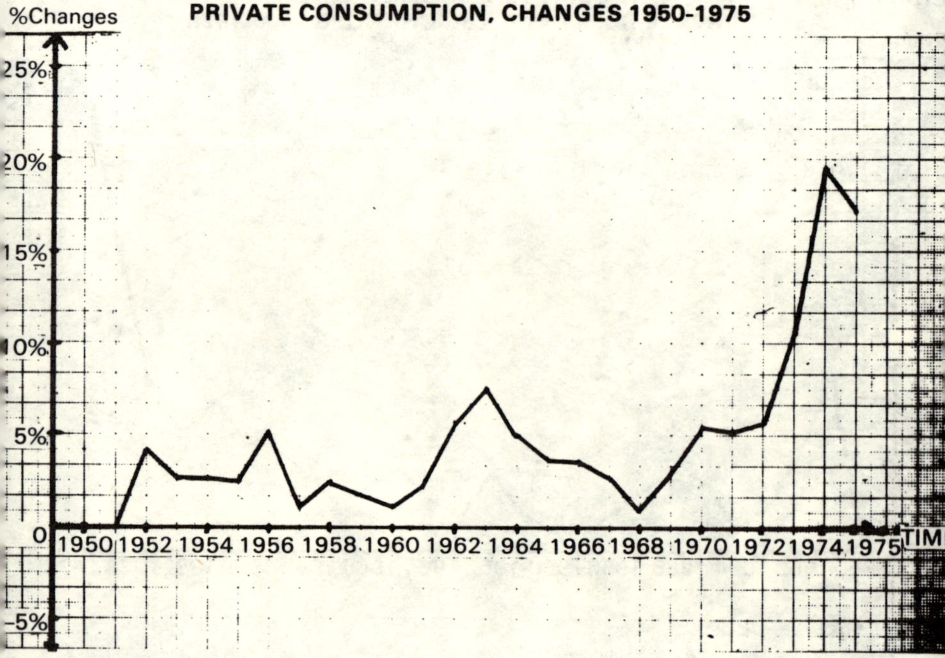

CHART 13(e)

FRANCE: PRICE INDICES OF PRIVATE CONSUMPTION, CHANGES, 1950-1975

%Change

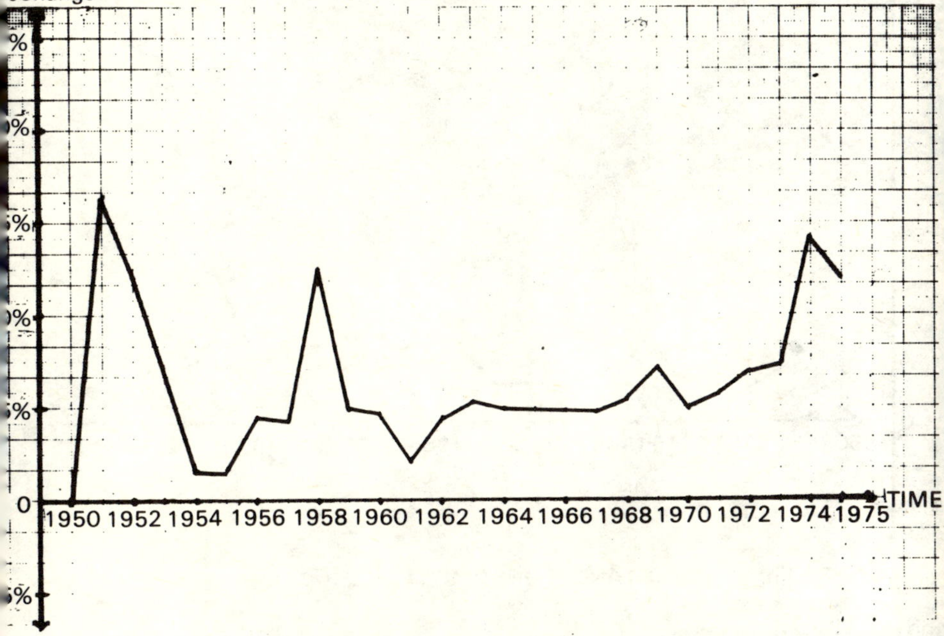

ART 13(f)

WEST GERMANY: PRICE INDICES OF PRIVATE CONSUMPTION, CHANGES 1950-1975

anges

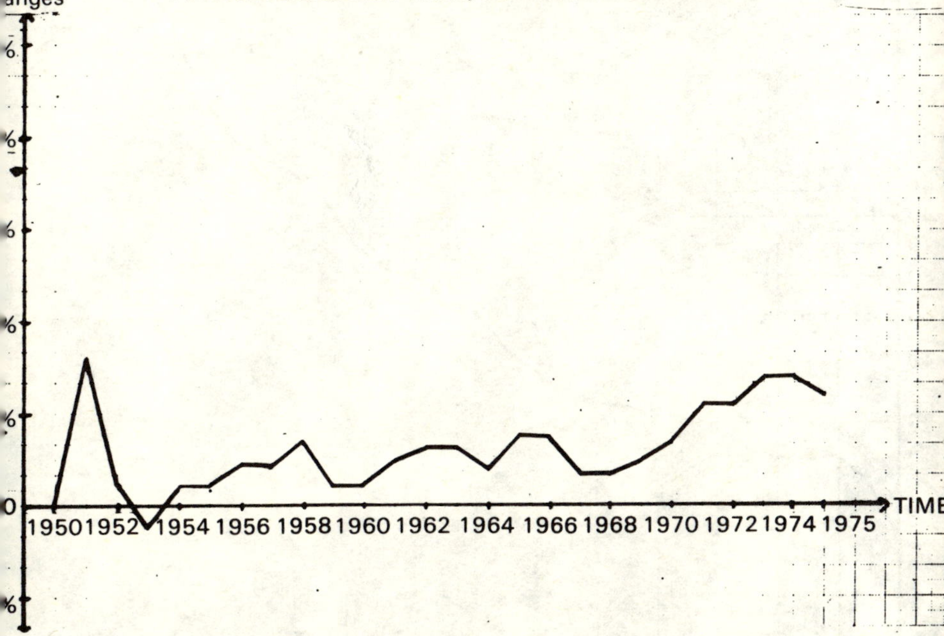

CHART 13(g)

NETHERLANDS: PRICE INDICES OF PRIVATE CONSUMPTION, CHANGES 1950-1975

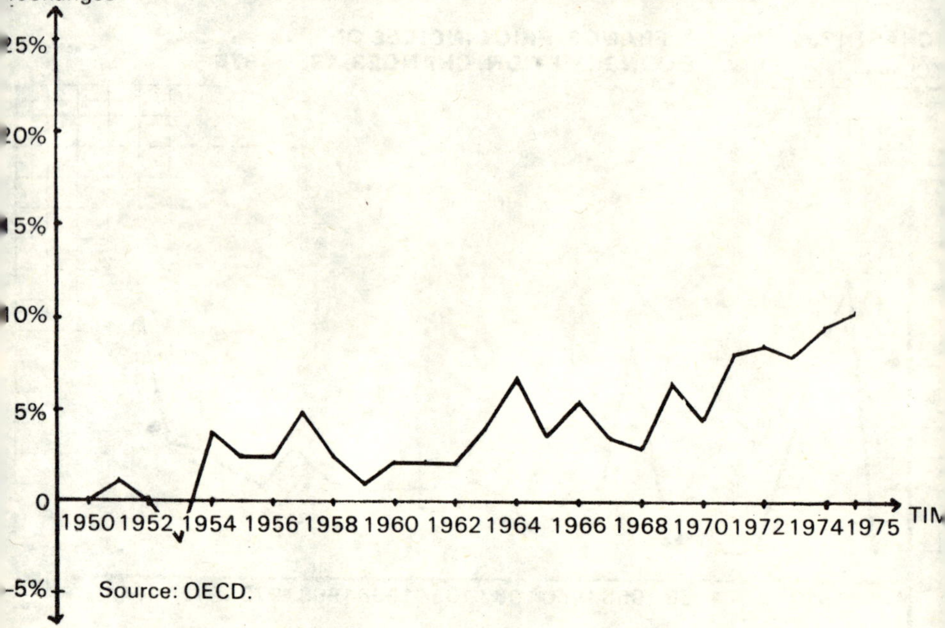

Source: OECD.

CHART 13(h)

ICELAND: CONSUMER PRICE INDEX

(1970 = 100)

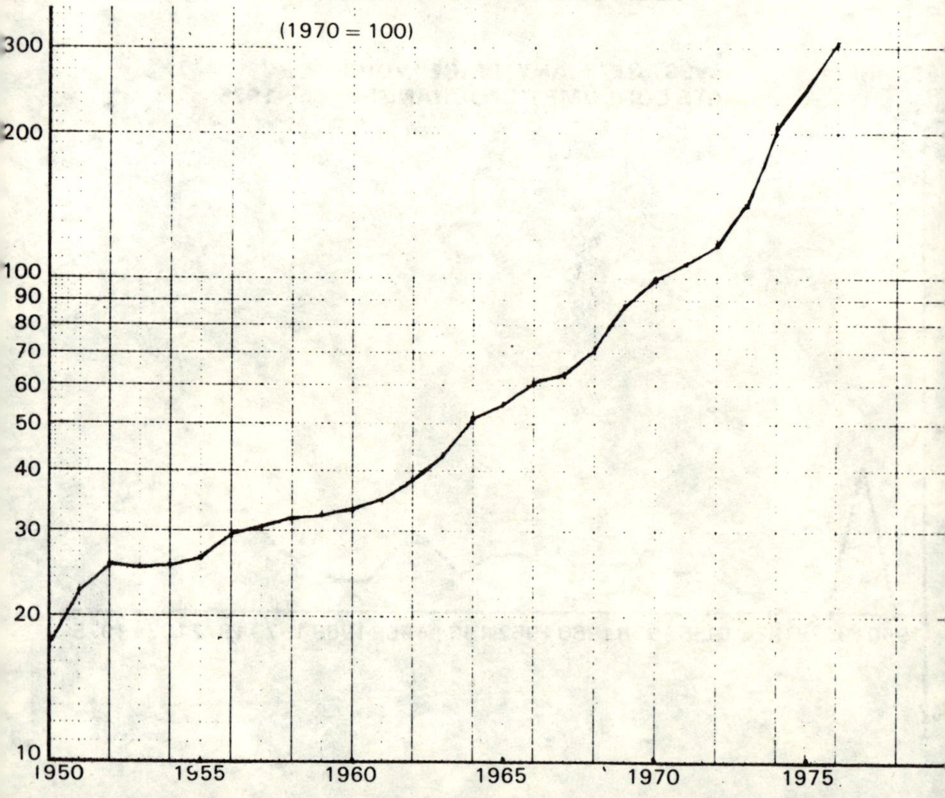

FIAT MONEY INFLATION IN FRANCE

Andrew Dickson White

Introduction

Andrew Dickson White, who achieved eminence as an historian, an educator, and a diplomat, was born in Homer, New York, on November 7, 1832. He graduated from Yale in 1853, studied at the Sorbonne in Paris in 1854 and at the University of Berlin in 1855 and 1856, meanwhile serving as attaché at the United States legation at St. Petersburg.

He became a professor of history at the University of Michigan when he was only twenty-five. The fraternity boys, on his arrival, thought him a freshman and lugged his bags to his hotel. But his teaching proved a revelation. As one of his students (Charles Kendall Adams) afterwards wrote of him: 'He not only instructed ... he inspired.'

From his freshman days he had dreamed of an American university more stately, more scholarly, and more free than any he had known. In 1867, with the help of an endowment from Ezra Cornell and a New York land grant, he established the present Cornell University at Ithaca, New York, and became its first president, a post which he held until 1885. He died November 4, 1918.

White was a man of affairs as well as a scholar. He served as United States minister to Germany from 1879 to 1881, as minister to Russia from 1892 to 1894, and as ambassador to Germany from 1897 to 1903. In 1899, he headed the American delegation to the Hague Peace Conference and was responsible for one of its most dramatic events – the celebration by the Americans of their Fourth of July by laying a laurel wreath on the tomb of Grotius, the father of international law.

The most famous of White's longer works is *A History of the*

Warfare of Science with Theology in Christendom, published in two volumes in 1896.

The short essay in the following pages was born of his lectures on the French Revolution. It was first publicly read before a meeting of Senators and members of the House of Representatives of both political parties at Washington on April 12, and before the Union League Club of New York on April 13, 1876. In 1912, at the age of eighty, at the request of a Canadian businessman, he revised and enlarged the essay 'for private circulation only.' It has since been republished several times and has become a classic.

What chiefly strikes today's reader is the astonishing similarity of the arguments put forward by our own contemporary inflationists to those of the inflationists of eighteenth-century France. Not less striking, of course, is the similarity in the actual consequences of paper money inflation in revolutionary France and inflation everywhere in the modern world.

These parallels were, of course, intentionally underlined by White. His essay was written not merely as a cold history, but as a lesson and a warning to his own American contemporaries. When his original lecture was read in 1876, the United States was still on a paper money standard, an inheritance from its resort to the Greenbacks during the Civil War. And though the Resumption Act had been passed on January 14, 1875, it was not until January 1, 1879 that gold payments were in fact resumed.

But these parallels strike us so forcibly today, not primarily because White underlined them for his hearers in 1876, but primarily because the course of inflation everywhere – economically, psychologically, politically, and morally – does in fact follow the same pattern.

Before we trace this pattern in more detail, we may pause to look at some connections, which White does not specifically refer to, between the fiat money inflation and the political chronology of the French Revolution. The States-General was called to meet on May 5, 1789 by Louis XVI, but defiantly adopted the title of the National Assembly on June 17. On July 14 came the storming of the Bastille. In April of 1790 came the first issue of 400,000,000 livres in paper money, followed by successive new issues.[1]

[1] A fuller chronology is appended at the end of White's essay in the present edition.

When the new Assembly met in October 1791, it contained such extremists as Robespierre, Danton, and Marat. On August 10, 1792, the mob stormed the royal palace, slaughtered the Swiss guards, and overthrew the monarchy. The massacres of September 1792 were followed by the trial and execution of Louis XVI in January 1793, and by the Reign of Terror. On February 28, 1793, at eight o'clock in the evening (as White records), a mob of men and women in disguise began plundering the stores and shops of Paris. And on September 29, 1793, came price-fixing – the Law of the Maximum, with its punishment of the guillotine for violators.

Now there is obviously a causal connection between these 'political' and 'economic policy' developments. And, as we study this, it becomes obvious that the causation was not merely one way. It was not merely the political terror that led to the monetary and price-fixing terror. The inauguration of inflation, by the obvious and fresh injustices that it brought about in the distribution of wealth and income, by the new burdens that it put upon underpaid labour, by causing the rise of a speculative and gambling class and the display of luxury by the new inflation-made rich, enormously increased envy, discontent, and resentment, and helped to accelerate and intensify the social upheaval and violence. Inflation aggravates the very evils it seeks to cure.

The most striking parallel between the events recorded in Andrew D. White's essay and the situation in the modern world is psychological. It is the persistence of delusions. The arguments of the inflationists, then and now, are essentially the same. The inflation in revolutionary France was begun to pay off a debt and finance a budgetary deficit. (The immediate cause of the French Revolution, in fact, was the bankrupt state of the public treasury, which forced Louis XVI to call the States-General.) Inflation was to be the 'short road to prosperity.' The great want of the country was thought to be a 'shortage' of the circulating medium. Merely add to the money supply, through the printing press, and all your difficulties dissolve. What the country needs is more 'purchasing power.' And as this remedy fails, and quite different results follow, the sole solution of the inflationists is still more money, still more 'purchasing power.'

The broad pattern of all inflations, historic and modern, is the same. The first result is commonly the 'recovery' that the inflationists, like others, are seeking. It is not until later that its disappointing and poisonous effects become apparent. The economic reasons for this are not obscure. When there is relative stagnation in business, and unemployment, it is usually because an unbalanced and unworkable relationship has developed between prices at which goods can be sold and their costs of production. The main difficulty, usually, is that wage-rates are too high in relation to prices. This could be cured by readjustment of specific wage-rates, by more flexible wages and prices, by permitting competition to work. The first effect of a new injection of bank credit or paper money into the system is, indeed, an apparent increase of that 'purchasing power' which is so much wanted. It enables 'surplus' goods to be sold at their existing prices. It enables prices of other goods to be raised to levels at which existing wage-rates can be paid and a full complement of workers hired. So it tends to restore that 'full employment' so cherished, at any cost, by the modern reformer. This goal is achieved under inflation by raising prices enough to validate the existing level of wages. But what is forgotten is that the adjustment could have been made not only just as well, but much better, by a realignment of the particular wages that had got out of line. Such piecemeal adjustment would have restored the necessary coordination of the price-and-wage structure without the subsequent evils and crises that the inflation is bound to produce.

Once 'full production' and 'full employment' have been restored, there is no further mixture of desired results with the damage that further inflation must do. *All* the results of inflation from that point on are necessarily harmful. If it raised all prices and all wages equally (which it doesn't), it would obviously benefit no one. It would merely force everybody to be a better mathematician; to think in higher figures; to get more for his own work but to pay more for everybody else's; to get a higher money income but to pay higher prices.

Even on this assumption of uniformity of price and wage increases, however, there would be one great evil effect. The real purchasing power of savings would be constantly eroded. All savers would be cheated. This would discourage thrift. It would discourage, in short, the creation of those savings which are necessary for the investment upon which all economic progress and increase of productivity depend.

This result may be put in another way. If the rise of prices and wages were uniform, the chief economic effect of inflation would be to benefit debtors at the expense of creditors. This, indeed, has been one of the main arguments for it in the past. It was a leading argument for it at the time of the French Revolution. But it is a glaring fallacy, especially in modern times, to identify debtors with the poor and creditors with the rich. In the United States today the chief debtors are the stockholders of the corporations. These stockholders are found among the wealthiest classes. The creditors include the direct bondholders of these same corporations (probably less wealthy, on the average, than the stockholders, for they include investors who cannot afford to take the stockholder's risks). The creditors also include the holders of life insurance policies, and of government bonds, large and small. They include millions of savings-bank depositors, made up mainly of people of moderate means.

A poor man never gets to be a big debtor. Only a rich man, or a man with a reputation of being rich, can get into that situation. It is economic nonsense today to talk of a 'debtor class' and a 'creditor class' as if these represented separate groups necessarily at different economic levels. Each of us is to some extent debtor, to some extent creditor. Even if it were possible to work out a statistical average, based on the net position of each of us, it is more than doubtful that the 'creditors' would prove on the average to be richer than the 'debtors'; it is much more probable that the relationship would prove to be the other way around. Nothing but injustice, discouragement of work and thrift, encouragement of speculation and gambling, and economic disruption can follow from an effort to swindle creditors at the expense of debtors by a constant lowering of the purchasing power of the monetary unit.

It is a mathematical truism, in fact, that once reasonably full employment has been achieved, by any means, any further inflation is bound to injure as many people as it profits. The gainers gain at the expense of the losers. Everyone whose product rises in price more than the average must gain at the expense of everyone whose product rises less than the average. Assuming unchanged physical production, anyone whose wage or salary advances more than the average must do so at the expense of everyone whose wage or salary goes up less than the average.

And inflation typically brings about just such alterations in the relative position of economic groups. Inflation always starts from a particular point. If the government prints more money to pay for war contracts, for example, the first beneficiaries are the government contractors. The next group of beneficiaries are the workers for these contractors. The third group is comprised of the tradesmen whom these workers patronize. Those whose incomes go up first can buy goods while prices are still low, and so gain an advantage. But others must pay higher prices for the goods they buy before their own goods or services have risen by an equivalent amount. These are the losers. So inflation disturbs and disrupts all pre-existing economic relationships.

It may be thought that, in one important aspect, the redistribution of real income and wealth brought about by modern inflations is less unjust than in inflations of the past. Some of our present inflationists even regard this redistribution as beneficent. White speaks repeatedly of the fact that in the assignat inflation 'everything was enormously inflated in price *except the wages of labour*.'

Now though this result was intensified at that time by the Law of the Maximum (which contained a provision that bound workers to their jobs by empowering the government to imprison those who refused to work), it appears to have been common to the older inflations. This result has been changed in our time by the existence of powerful unions, many of which are able to impose 'escalator' clauses in their contracts which provide not only for automatic wage increases proportionate to increases in the official cost-of-living index, but for automatic 'annual improvement' increases on top of these. Other unions are also able, by strikes and violence, to impose wage increases that go beyond both consumer-price increases and any increase in marginal labour productivity.

This has led some academic inflationists in our time to conclude that 'creeping inflation probably prevents more injustice than it creates.' 'Labour,' as they see it, is gaining by the process. And is not any inflation beneficent that gives more to the 'poor' and to the 'underdog'?

Such a view is superficial and false. Its initial mistake is to treat labour as one huge monolithic lump. Actually, wages in each of scores of major industries differ sharply from each other. They are changed at different times and to different degrees. Within each industry there are scores of different classifications of workers. And there are millions of unorganized or salary workers whose compensation is fixed by individual bargains. Coercive union bargaining not only raises the wages of a minority of organized labour at the expense of the greater body of unorganized labour, but it raises the wages of the union workers in more strategic positions at the expense of the union workers in less strategic positions. It does this by forcing up the prices of the goods that the less-advantaged workers must buy, faster than they can force up their own wages. (Net profit margins, contrary to common opinion, constitute a minor element in prices. Corporate profits after taxes in 1958, for example, were only five per cent of the national income.) It should be mathematically obvious that in the long run wages that are raised above the average must be raised at the expense of those that are raised less than the average. And experience shows that it is the workers who are already among the highest paid who are usually able by their stronger organization to increase their advantage at the further expense of the lower-paid.

Even this does not tell the full story. The unions that succeed in raising their wages beyond the point of marginal productivity do so only at the expense of bringing about unemployment in their own ranks. Those who retain their jobs at the new higher wage do so at the expense of their colleagues who have been dropped.

The effect of all this is to put still greater political pressure on the government to resort to still further money-and-credit inflation in order to raise prices to make 'full employment' possible at the higher wage rates. But where there are extensive automatic wage-escalator clauses this becomes a wild accelerative spiral (like that following the practically universalized escalator wage clauses in Germany in 1923) that fails to cure the unemployment and leads only to a catastrophe.

All this explains why, following the first stage of a recovery (assuming that this recovery occurs), there can be no further productive stimulation from inflation, but at best a redistribution of income and wealth. A point is soon reached, however, where there is a net profit in inflation for fewer and fewer people and a net loss for more and more, until we reach a point where the profit is taken out of inflation for nearly everybody. This is because the kind of production stimulated by inflation even at the beginning is an unbalanced production (owing to the money illusions that inflation creates) and because inflation finally encourages merely malinvestment, thriftlessness, speculation, and gambling at the expense of production itself.

White points out in his account that, after the first stimulation following the early issue of new assignats, there were periods of prostration and renewed complaints of 'shortage of money.' The economic explanation of this is simple. The value of money, like the value of everything else, is determined chiefly by the quantity of it in existence. The more wheat there is, the less the value of an individual bushel of wheat; the more money in circulation, the lower the purchasing power of an individual unit.

But the value of the monetary unit does not fall, contrary to a common assumption, in exact proportion to the increase in the total quantity of money in circulation. When the quantity is at first increased, the individual unit of money commonly loses its value much more slowly than the quantity of money increases. This means that more goods are bought with the increased money supply, and we get the familiar stimulation and recovery of the first stages of an inflation. But as the supply of money continues to be increased, a fear begins to spread that there will be still further increases. It begins to be believed that the value of the monetary unit is going to continue to fall – that it will be less next year than this year, less next month than this month. Once such a belief has taken hold, the decline in the value of the monetary unit is *anticipated.* The value of the monetary unit begins to fall *faster* than the supply is or can be increased.

The monetary managers are from then on in a necessarily losing battle. The more they increase the supply of money, the more public opinion anticipates still further increases. Prices then go up *more* than in proportion to the increase in the money supply. The new increased supplies of money therefore do a *smaller* volume of business and have a lower *total* value than the previous smaller supplies of money. Then comes the characteristic complaint, which White writes about, of a 'shortage of money.' The more desperately the monetary managers try to offset this shortage by further issues of bills, the more the public fears for the value of the monetary unit, the more the monetary unit falls, and the greater the shortage of money becomes. White writes, on his last pages, of the *'law of accelerating issue and depreciation.'* This is the psychological and economic explanation of that law.

Inflation, in its final stages, always ends in prostration, in what modern economists call a 'stabilization crisis.' The explanation of this stabilization crisis is not mysterious. During the inflation, as we have just seen, prices do not respond in simple proportionality to the increase in the money supply. Some prices race beyond this, *anticipating* a further inflation. Even if the inflation is halted at some point and no deflation sets in – that is, even if the increased supply of money is merely locked where it is and not reduced – the stabilization crisis sets in because these anticipatory prices collapse. This stabilization crisis, like the drunkard's hangover, is part of the price that must be paid for every inflationary orgy.

The story that Andrew D. White tells is complete in itself. It carries its own moral. But just as the French of 1790 had failed to learn the lessons of the inflation of seventy years before, in John Law's time, so the present-day world has failed to learn the lesson of the assignats.

Perhaps the study of other great inflations – of John Law's experiments with credit in France between 1716 and 1720; of the history of our own American currency between 1775 and 1780; of the Greenbacks of our Civil War; of the great German inflation which culminated in 1923 – would help to underscore and impress that lesson. Must we, from this appalling and repeated record, draw once more the despairing conclusion that the only thing man learns from history is that man learns nothing from history? Or have we still time enough, and sense enough, and courage enough, to be guided by these dreadful lessons of the past?

Henry Hazlitt
New York City
March 1959

FIAT MONEY INFLATION IN FRANCE

How It Came

Early in the year 1789 the French nation found itself in deep financial embarrassment: there was a heavy debt and a serious deficit.

The vast reforms of that period, though a lasting blessing politically, were a temporary evil financially. There was a general want of confidence in business circles; capital had shown its proverbial timidity by retiring out of sight as far as possible; throughout the land was stagnation.

Statesmanlike measures, careful watching, and wise management would, doubtless, have ere long led to a return of confidence, a reappearance of money, and a resumption of business; but these involved patience and self-denial, and, thus far in human history, these are the rarest products of political wisdom. Few nations have ever been able to exercise these virtues; and France was not then one of these few.

There was a general search for some short road to prosperity: ere long the idea was set afloat that the great want of the country was more of the circulating medium; and this was speedily followed by calls for an issue of paper money. The Minister of Finance at this period was Necker. In financial ability he was acknowledged as among the great bankers of Europe, but his was something more than financial ability: he had a deep feeling of patriotism and a high sense of personal honour. The difficulties in his way were great, but he steadily endeavoured to keep France faithful to those principles in monetary affairs which the general experience of modern times had found the only path to national safety. As difficulties arose, the National Assembly drew away from him, and soon came among the members renewed suggestions of paper money: orators in public meetings, at the clubs, and in the Assembly, proclaimed it a panacea – a way of 'securing resources without paying interest.' Journalists caught it up and displayed its beauties, among these men, Marat, who, in his newspaper, 'The Friend of the People,' also joined the cries against Necker, picturing him – a man of sterling honesty, who gave up health and fortune for the sake of France – as a wretch seeking only to enrich himself from the public purse.

Against this tendency toward the issue of irredeemable paper Necker contended as best he might. He knew well to what it always had led, even when surrounded by the most skilful guarantees. Among those who struggled to support ideas similar to his was Bergasse, a deputy from Lyons, whose pamphlets, then and later, against such issues exerted a wider influence, perhaps, than any others. Parts of them seem fairly inspired. Anyone today reading his prophecies of the evils sure to follow such a currency would certainly ascribe to him a miraculous foresight, were it not so clear that his prophetic power was due simply to a knowledge of natural laws revealed by history.

But this current in favour of paper money became so strong that an effort was made to breast it by a compromise; and during the last months of 1789 and the first months of 1790 came discussions in the National Assembly looking to issues of notes based upon the landed property of the Church, which was to be confiscated for that purpose. But care was to be taken; the issue was to be largely in the shape of notes of 1,000, 300, and 200 livres,* too large to be used as ordinary currency, but of convenient size to be used in purchasing the Church lands; besides this, they were to bear interest and this would tempt holders to hoard them. The Assembly thus held back from issuing smaller obligations.

Remembrances of the ruin which had come from the great issues of smaller currency at an earlier day were still vivid. Yet the pressure toward a popular currency for universal use grew stronger and stronger. The finance committee of the Assembly reported that 'the people demand a new circulating medium'; that 'the circulation of paper money is the best of operations'; that 'it is the most free because it reposes on the will of the people'; that 'it will bind the interest of the citizens to the public good.'

The report appealed to the patriotism of the French people with the following exhortation: 'Let us show to Europe that we understand our own resources; let us immediately take the broad

*Editor's Note: The livre was the common coin of exchange in France at the beginning of the period White describes. The franc became the official monetary unit in 1795, with conversion at the rate of 81 livres to 80 francs.

road to our liberation instead of dragging ourselves along the tortuous and obscure paths of fragmentary loans.' It concluded by recommending an issue of paper money carefully guarded, to the full amount of four hundred million livres, and the argument was pursued until the objection to smaller notes faded from view.

Typical in the debate on the whole subject, in its various phases, were the declarations of M. Matrineau. He was loud and long for paper money, his only fear being that the Committee had not authorized enough of it; he declared that business was stagnant, and that the sole cause was a want of more of the circulating medium; that paper money ought to be made a legal tender; that the Assembly should rise above prejudices which the failures of John Law's paper money had caused, several decades before. Like every supporter of irredeemable paper money then or since, he seemed to think that the laws of Nature had changed since previous disastrous issues. He said: 'Paper money under a despotism is dangerous; it favours corruption; but in a nation constitutionally governed, which itself takes care in the emission of its notes, which determines their number and use, that danger no longer exists.' He insisted that John Law's notes at first restored prosperity, but that the wretchedness and ruin they caused resulted from their overissue, and that such an overissue is possible only under a despotism.[2]

M. de la Rochefoucauld gave his opinion that 'the assignats will draw specie out of the coffers where it is now hoarded.'[3]

On the other hand, Cazalès and Maury showed that the result could only be disastrous. Never, perhaps, did a political prophecy meet with more exact fulfillment in every line than the terrible picture drawn in one of Cazalès' speeches in this debate. Still the current ran stronger and stronger; Petion made a brilliant oration in favour of the report, and Necker's influence and experience were gradually worn away.

Mingled with the financial argument was a strong political plea. The National Assembly had determined to confiscate the vast real property of the French Church – the pious accumulations of fifteen hundred years. There were princely estates in the country, bishops' palaces, and conventual buildings in the towns; these formed between one-fourth and one-third of the entire real property of France, and amounted in value to at least two thousand million livres. By a few sweeping strokes all this became the property of the nation. Never, apparently, did a government secure a more solid basis for a great financial future.[4]

There were two special reasons why French statesmen desired speedily to sell these lands. First, a financial reason – to obtain money to relieve the government. Secondly, a political reason – to get this land distributed among the thrifty middle classes, and so commit them to the Revolution and to the government which gave their title.

It was urged, then, that the issue of four hundred millions of paper, (not in the shape of interest-bearing bonds, as had at first been proposed, but in notes small as well as large), would give the treasury something to pay out immediately, and relieve the national necessities; that, having been put into circulation, this paper money would stimulate business; that it would give to all capitalists, large or small, the means for buying from the nation the ecclesiastical real estate; and that from the proceeds of this real estate the nation would pay its debts and also obtain new funds for new necessities. Never was theory more seductive both to financiers and statesmen.

It would be a great mistake to suppose that the statesmen of France, or the French people, were ignorant of the dangers in issuing irredeemable paper money. No matter how skillfully the bright side of such a currency was exhibited, all thoughtful men in France remembered its dark side. They knew too well, from that ruinous experience, seventy years before, in John Law's time, the difficulties and dangers of a currency not well based and controlled. They had then learned how easy it is to issue it; how difficult it is to check its overissue; how seductively it leads to the absorption of the means of the workingmen and men of small fortunes; how heavily it falls on all those living on fixed incomes, salaries, or wages; how securely it creates on the ruins of the prosperity of all men of meager means a class of debauched speculators, the most injurious class that a nation can harbour – more injurious, indeed, than professional criminals whom the law recognizes and can throttle; how it stimulates overproduction at first and leaves every industry flaccid afterward; how it breaks down thrift and develops political and social immorality. All this France had been thoroughly taught by experience. Many then living had felt the result of such an experiment – the issues of paper money under John Law, a man who to this day is acknowledged one of the most ingenious financiers the world has ever known; and there were then sitting in the National Assembly of France many who owed the poverty of their families to those issues of paper. Hardly a man in the country who had not heard those who issued it cursed as the authors of the most frightful catastrophe France had then experienced.[5]

It was no mere attempt at theatrical display, but a natural impulse, which led a thoughtful statesman, during the debate, to hold up a piece of that old paper money and to declare that it was stained with the blood and tears of their fathers.

And it would also be a mistake to suppose that the National Assembly, which discussed this matter, was composed of mere wild revolutionists; no inference could be more wide of the fact. Whatever may have been the character of the men who legislated for France afterward, no thoughtful student of history can deny, despite all the arguments and sneers of reactionary statesmen and historians, that few more keen-sighted legislative bodies have ever met than this first French Constitutional Assembly. In it were such men as Sieyès, Bailly, Necker, Mirabeau, Talleyrand, Du Pont de Nemours, and a multitude of others who, in various sciences and in the political world, had already shown and were destined afterward to show themselves among the strongest and shrewdest men that Europe has yet seen.

But the current toward paper money had become irresistible. It was constantly urged, and with a great show of force, that if any nation could safely issue it, France was now that nation; that she was fully warned by her severe experience under John Law; that she was now a constitutional government, controlled by an enlightened, patriotic people – not, as in the days of the former issues of paper money, an absolute monarchy controlled by politicians and adventurers; that she was able to secure every livre of her paper money by a virtual mortgage on a landed domain vastly greater in value than the entire issue; that, with men like Bailly, Mirabeau, and Necker at her head, she could not commit the financial mistakes and crimes from which France had suffered under John Law, the Regent Duke of Orleans, and Cardinal Dubois.

Oratory prevailed over science and experience. In April 1790, came the final decree to issue four hundred millions of livre in paper money, based upon confiscated property of the Church for its security. The deliberations on this first decree and on the bill carrying it into effect were most interesting; prominent in the debate being Necker, Du Pont de Nemours, Maury, Cazalès, Petion, Bailly, and many others hardly inferior. The discussions were certainly very able; no person can read them at length in the *Moniteur*, nor even in the summaries of the parliamentary history, without feeling that various modern historians have done wretched injustice to those men who were then endeavouring to stand between France and ruin.

This sum – four hundred millions, so vast in those days – was issued in assignats, which were notes secured by a pledge of productive real estate and bearing interest to the holder at three per cent. No irredeemable currency has ever claimed a more scientific and practical guarantee for its goodness and for its proper action on public finances. On the one hand, it had what the world recognized as a most practical security – a mortgage on productive real estate of vastly greater value than the issue. On the other hand, as the notes bore interest, there seemed cogent reason for their being withdrawn from circulation whenever they became redundant.[6]

As speedily as possible the notes were put into circulation. Unlike those issued in John Law's time, they were engraved in the best style of the art. To stimulate loyalty, the portrait of the King was placed in the centre; to arouse public spirit, patriotic legends and emblems surrounded it; to stimulate public cupidity, the amount of interest which the note would yield each day to the holder was printed in the margin; and the whole was duly garnished with stamps and signatures to show that it was carefully registered and controlled.[7]

To crown its work the National Assembly, to explain the advantages of this new currency, issued an address to the French people. In this address it spoke of the nation as 'delivered by this grand means from all uncertainty and from all ruinous results of the credit system.' It foretold that this issue 'would bring back into the public treasury, into commerce, and into all branches of industry, strength, abundance, and prosperity.'[8]

Some of the arguments in this address are worth recalling, and, among them, the following: 'Paper money is without inherent value unless it represents some special property. Without representing some special property it is inadmissible in trade to compete with a metallic currency, which has a value real and independent of the public action; therefore it is that the paper money which has only the public authority as its basis has always caused ruin where it has been established; that is the reason why the bank notes of 1720, issued by John Law, after having caused terrible evils, have left only frightful memories. Therefore it is that the National Assembly has not wished to expose you to this danger, but has given this new paper money not only a value derived from the national authority but a value real and immutable, a value which permits it to sustain advantageously a competition with the precious metals themselves.'[9]

But the final declaration was, perhaps, the most interesting. It was as follows:

'These assignats, bearing interest as they do, will soon be considered better than the coin now hoarded, and will bring it out again into circulation.' The King, was also induced to issue a proclamation recommending that his people receive this new money without objection.

All this caused great joy. Among the various utterances of this feeling was the letter of M. Sarot, directed to the editor of the *Journal of the National Assembly*, and scattered through France. M. Sarot is hardly able to contain himself as he anticipates the prosperity and glory that this issue of paper is to bring to his country. One thing only vexes him, and that is the pamphlet of M. Bergasse against the assignats; therefore it is after a long series of arguments and protestations, in order to give a final proof of his confidence in the paper money and his entire skepticism as to the evils predicted by Bergasse and others, M. Sarot solemnly lays his house, garden, and furniture upon the altar of his country and offers to sell them for paper money alone.

There were, indeed, some gainsayers. These especially appeared among the clergy, who, naturally, abhorred the confiscation of Church property. Various ecclesiastics made speeches, some of them full of pithy and weighty arguments, against the proposed issue of paper, and there is preserved a sermon from one priest threatening all persons handling the new money with eternal damnation. But the great majority of the French people, who had suffered ecclesiastical oppression so long, regarded these utterances as the wriggling of a fish on the hook, and enjoyed the sport all the better.[10]

The first result of this issue was apparently all that the most sanguine could desire: the treasury was at once greatly relieved; a portion of the public debt was paid; creditors were encouraged; credit revived; ordinary expenses were met, and, a considerable part of this paper money having thus been passed from the government into the hands of the people, trade increased and all difficulties seemed to vanish. The anxieties of Necker, the prophecies of Maury and Cazalès seemed proven utterly futile. And, indeed, it is quite possible that, if the national authorities had stopped with this issue, few of the financial evils which afterwards arose would have been severely felt; the four hundred millions of paper money then issued would have simply discharged the function of a similar amount of specie. But soon there came another result: times grew less easy; by the end of September, within five months after the issue of the four hundred millions in assignats, the government had spent them and was again in distress.[11]

The old remedy immediately and naturally recurred to the minds of men. Throughout the country began a cry for another issue of paper; thoughtful men then began to recall what their fathers had told them about the seductive path of paper-money issues in John Law's time, and to remember the prophecies that they themselves had heard in the debate on the first issue of assignats less than six months before.

At that time the opponents of paper had prophesied that, once on the downward path of inflation, the nation could not be restrained and that more issues would follow. The supporters of the first issue had asserted that this was a calumny, that *the people* were now in control, and that they could and would check these issues whenever they desired.

The condition of opinion in the Assembly was, therefore, chaotic: a few schemers and dreamers were loud and outspoken for paper money; many of the more shallow and easy-going were inclined to yield; the more thoughtful endeavoured to breast the current.

One man there was who could have withstood the pressure: Mirabeau. He was the popular idol – the great orator of the Assembly and much more than a great orator – he had carried the nation through some of its worst dangers by a boldness almost godlike; in the various conflicts he had shown not only oratorical boldness, but amazing foresight. As to his real opinion on an irredeemable currency there can be no doubt. It was the opinion which all true statesmen have held, before his time and since – in his own country, in England, in America, in every modern civilized nation. In his letter to Cerutti, written in January 1789, hardly six months before, he had spoken of paper money as 'a nursery of tyranny, corruption, and delusion; a veritable debauch of authority in delirium.' In one of his early speeches in the National Assembly he had called such money, when Anson covertly suggested its issue, 'a loan to an armed robber,' and said of it: 'That infamous word, paper money, ought to be banished from our language.' In his private letters written at this very time, which were revealed at a later period, he showed that he was fully aware of the dangers of inflation. But he yielded to the pressure: partly because he thought it important to sell the government lands rapidly to the people, and so develop speedily a large class of small landholders pledged to stand by the government which gave them their titles; partly, doubtless, from a love of immediate rather than of remote applause; and, generally, in a vague hope that the severe, inexorable laws of finance which had brought heavy punishments upon governments emitting an irredeemable currency in other lands, at other times, might in some way at this time be warded off from France.[12]

The question was brought up by Montesquieu's report on August 27, 1790. This report favoured, with evident reluctance, an additional issue of paper. It went on to declare that the original issue of four hundred millions, though opposed at the beginning, had proved successful; that assignats were economical, though they had dangers; and, as a climax, came the declaration: 'We must save the country.'[13]

Upon this report Mirabeau then made one of his most powerful speeches. He confessed that he had at first feared the issue of assignats, but that he now dared urge it; that experience had shown the issue of paper money most serviceable; that the report proved the first issue of assignats a success; that public affairs had come out of distress; the ruin had been averted and credit established. He then argued that there was a difference between paper money of the recent issue and that from which the nation had suffered so much in John Law's time; he declared that the French nation had now become enlightened and he added, 'Deceptive subtleties can no longer mislead patriots and men of sense in this matter.' He then went on to say: 'We must accomplish that which we have begun,' and declared that there must be one more large issue of paper, guaranteed by the national lands and by the good faith of the French nation.

To show how practical the system was he insisted that just as soon as paper money should become too abundant it would be absorbed in rapid purchases of national lands; and he made a very striking comparison between this self-adjusting, self-converting system and the rains descending in showers upon the earth, then in swelling rivers discharged into the sea, then drawn up in vapour and finally scattered over the earth again in rapidly fertilizing showers. He predicted that the members would be surprised at the astonishing success of this paper money and that there would be none too much of it.

His theory grew by what it fed upon – as the paper-money theory has generally done. Toward the close, in a burst of eloquence, he suggested that assignats be created to an amount sufficient to cover the national debt, and that all the national lands be exposed for sale immediately, predicting that thus prosperity would return to the nation and that all classes would find this additional issue of paper money a blessing.[14]

This speech was frequently interrupted by applause; a unanimous vote ordered it printed, and copies were spread throughout France. The impulse given by it permeated all subsequent discussion; Gouy arose and proposed to liquidate the national debt of twenty-four hundred millions – to use his own words – 'by one single operation, grand, simple, magnificent.'[15] This 'operation' was to be the emission of twenty-four hundred millions in legal tender notes, and a law that specie should not be accepted in purchasing national lands. His demagogy bloomed forth magnificently. He advocated an appeal to the people, who, to use his flattering expression, 'ought alone to give the law in a matter so interesting.' The newspapers of the period, in reporting his speech, noted it with the very significant remark, 'This discourse was loudly applauded.'

To him replied Brillat-Savarin. He called attention to the depreciation of assignats already felt. He tried to make the Assembly see that natural laws work as inexorably in France as elsewhere; he predicted that if this new issue were made, there would come a depreciation of thirty per cent. Singular, that the man who so fearlessly stood against this tide of unreason has left to the world simply a reputation as the most brilliant cook that ever existed! He was followed by the Abbe Goutes, who declared – what seems grotesque to those who have read the history of an irredeemable paper currency in any country – that new issues of paper money 'will supply a circulating medium which will protect public morals from corruption.'[16]

Into this debate was brought a report by Necker. He was not, indeed, the great statesman whom France especially needed at this time, of all times. He did not recognize the fact that the nation was entering a great revolution, but he could and did see that, come what might, there were simple principles of finance which must be adhered to. Most earnestly, therefore, he endeavoured to dissuade the Assembly from the proposed issue, suggesting that other means could be found for accomplishing the result, and he predicted terrible evils. But the current was running too fast. The only result was that Necker was spurned as a man of the past; he sent in his resignation and left France forever.[17] The paper-money demagogues shouted for joy at his departure; their chorus rang through the journalism of the time. No words could express their contempt for a man who was unable to see the advantages of filling the treasury with the issues of a printing press. Marat, Hébert, Camille Desmoulins, and the whole mass of demagogues so soon to follow them to the guillotine were especially jubilant.[18]

Continuing the debate, Rewbell attacked Necker, saying that the assignats were not at par because there were not yet enough of them; he insisted that payments for public lands be received in assignats alone; and suggested that the church bells of the kingdom be melted down into small money. Le Brun attacked the whole scheme in the Assembly, as he had done in the Committee, declaring that the proposal, instead of relieving the nation, would wreck it. The papers of the time very significantly say that at this there arose many murmurs. Chabroud came to the rescue. He said that the issue of assignats would relieve the distress of the people, and he presented very neatly the new theory of paper money and its basis in the following words: 'The earth is the source of value; you cannot distribute the earth in a circulating value, but this paper becomes representative of that value and it is evident that the creditors of the nation will not be injured by taking it.' On the other hand, appeared in the leading paper, the *Moniteur*, a very thoughtful article against paper money, which sums up all by saying, 'It is, then, evident that all paper which cannot, at the will of the bearer, be converted into specie cannot discharge the functions of money.' This article goes on to cite Mirabeau's former opinion in his letter to Cerutti, published in 1789 – the famous opinion of paper money as 'a nursery of tyranny, corruption, and delusion; a veritable debauch of authority in delirium.' Lablache, in the Assembly, quoted a saying that 'paper money is the emetic of great states.'[19]

Boutidoux, resorting to phrasemaking, called the assignats *'un papier terre,'* or 'land converted into paper.' Boislandry answered vigorously and foretold evil results. Pamphlets continued to be issued, among them, one so pungent that it was brought into the Assembly and read there – the truth which it presented with great clearness being simply that doubling the quantity of money or substitutes for money in a nation simply increases prices, disturbs values, alarms capital, diminishes legitimate enterprise, and so decreases the demand both for products and for labour; that the only persons to be helped by it are the rich who have large debts to pay. This pamphlet was signed, 'A Friend of the People,' and was received with great applause by the thoughtful minority in the Assembly. Du Pont de Nemours, who had stood by Necker in the debate on the first issue of assignats, arose, avowed the pamphlet to be his, and said sturdily that he had always voted against the emission of irredeemable paper and always would.[20]

Far more important than any other argument against inflation was the speech of Talleyrand. He had been among the boldest and most radical French statesmen. He it was – a former bishop – who, more than any other, had carried the extreme measure of taking into the possession of the nation the great landed estates of the Church, and he had supported the first issue of four hundred millions. But he now adopted a judicial tone – attempted to show to the Assembly the very simple truth that the effect of a second issue of assignats may be different from that of the first; that the first was evidently needed; that the second may be as injurious as the first was useful. He exhibited various weak points in the inflation fallacies and presented forcibly the trite truth that no laws and no decrees can keep large issues of irredeemable paper at par with specie.

In his speech occur these words; 'You can, indeed, arrange it so that the people shall be forced to take a thousand livres in paper for a thousand livres in specie; but you can never arrange it so that a man shall be obliged to give a thousand livres in specie for a thousand livres in paper – in that fact is embedded the entire question; and on account of that fact the whole system fails.'[21]

The nation at large now began to take part in the debate; thoughtful men saw that here was the turning point between good and evil; that the nation stood at the parting of the ways. Most of the great commercial cities bestirred themselves and sent up remonstrances against the new emission, twenty-five being opposed and seven in favour of it.

But eloquent theorists arose to glorify paper and among these, Royer, who on September 14, 1790, put forth a pamphlet entitled *Reflections of a Patriotic Citizen on the Issue of Assignats*, in which he gave many specious reasons why the assignats could not be depressed, and spoke of the argument against them as 'vile clamours of people bribed to affect public opinion.' He said to the National Assembly, 'If it is necessary to create five thousand millions, and more, of the paper, decree such a creation gladly.' He, too, predicted, as many others had done, a time when gold was to lose all its value, since all exchanges would be made with this admirable, guaranteed paper, and therefore that coin would come out from the places where it was hoarded. He foretold prosperous times to France in case these great issues of paper were continued and declared these 'the only means to insure happiness, glory, and liberty to the French nation.' Speeches like this gave courage to a new swarm of theorists. It began to be especially noted that men who had never shown any ability to make or increase fortunes for themselves abounded in brilliant plans for creating and increasing wealth for the country at large.

Greatest force of all, on September 27, 1790, came Mirabeau's final speech. The most sober and conservative of his modern opponents speaks of its eloquence as 'prodigious.' In this the great orator dwelt first on the political necessity involved, declaring that the most pressing need was to get the government lands into the hands of the people, and so to commit to the nation and against the old privileged classes the class of landholders thus created.

Through the whole course of his arguments there is one leading point enforced with all his eloquence and ingenuity – the excellence of the proposed currency, its stability, and its security. He declares that, being based on the pledge of public lands and convertible into them, the notes are better secured than if redeemable in specie; that the precious metals are only employed in the secondary arts, while the French paper money represents the first and most real of all property, the source of all production, *the land*; that while other nations have been obliged to emit paper money, none have ever been so fortunate as the French nation, for the reason that none had ever before been able to give this landed security; that whoever takes French paper money has practically a mortgage to secure it – and on landed property which can easily be sold to satisfy his claims, while other nations have been able only to give a vague claim on the entire nation. 'And,' he cries, 'I would rather have a mortgage on a garden than on a kingdom!'

Other arguments of his are more demagogical. He declares that the only interests affected will be those of bankers and capitalists, but that manufacturers will see prosperity restored to them. Some of his arguments seem almost puerile, as when he says, 'If gold has been hoarded through timidity or malignity, the issue of paper will show that gold is not necessary, and it will then come forth.' But, as a whole, the speech was brilliant; it was often interrupted by applause; it settled the question. People did not stop to consider that it was the dashing speech of an orator and not the matured judgment of a financial expert; they did not see that calling Mirabeau or Talleyrand to advise upon a monetary policy, because they had shown boldness in danger and strength in conflict, was like summoning a prize fighter to mend a watch.

In vain did Maury show that, while the first issues of John Law's paper had brought prosperity, those that followed brought misery; in vain did he quote from a book published in John Law's time, showing that Law was at first considered a patriot and friend of humanity; in vain did he hold up to the Assembly one of Law's bills and appeal to their memories of the wretchedness brought upon France by them; in vain did Du Pont present a simple and really wise plan of substituting notes in the payment of the floating debt which should not form a part of the ordinary circulating medium; nothing could resist the eloquence of Mirabeau. Barnave, following, insisted that 'Law's paper was based upon the phantoms of the Mississippi; ours, upon the solid basis of ecclesiastical lands,' and he proved that the assignats could not depreciate further. Prudhomme's newspaper poured contempt over gold as security for the currency, extolled real estate as the only true basis, and was fervent in praise of the convertibility and self-adjusting features of the proposed scheme.

In spite of all this plausibility and eloquence, a large minority stood firm to their earlier principles; but on September 29, 1790, by a vote of 508 to 423, the deed was done; a bill was passed authorizing the issue of eight hundred millions of new assignats, but solemnly declaring that in no case should the entire amount put in circulation exceed twelve hundred millions. To make assurance doubly sure, it also provided that as fast as the assignats were paid into the treasury for land they should be burned, and thus a healthful contraction be constantly maintained. Unlike the first issue, these new notes were to bear no interest.[22]

Great were the plaudits of the nation at this relief. Among the multitudes of pamphlets expressing this joy which have come down to us the *Friend of the Revolution* is the most interesting. It begins as follows: 'Citizens, the deed is done. The assignats are the keystone of the arch. It has just been happily put in position. Now I can announce to you that the Revolution is finished and there only remain one or two important questions. All the rest is but a matter of detail which cannot deprive us any longer of the pleasure of admiring this important work in its entirety. The provinces and the commercial cities which were at first alarmed at the proposal to issue so much paper money now send expressions of their thanks; specie is coming out to be joined with paper money. Foreigners come to us from all parts of Europe to seek their happiness under laws which they admire; and soon France, enriched by her new property and by the national industry which is preparing for fruitfulness, will demand still another creation of paper money.'

France was now fully committed to a policy of inflation; and, if there had been any question of this before, all doubts were removed now by various acts very significant as showing the exceeding difficulty of stopping a nation once in the full tide of a depreciating currency. The National Assembly had from the first shown an amazing liberality to all sorts of enterprises, wise or foolish, which were urged 'for the good of the people.' As a result of these and other largesses, the old cry of the 'lack of a circulating medium' broke forth again; and especially loud were the clamours for more small bills. The cheaper currency had largely driven out the dearer; paper had caused small silver and copper money mainly to disappear; all sorts of notes of hand, circulating under the name of 'confidence bills,' flooded France – sixty-three kinds in Paris alone.

This unguaranteed currency caused endless confusion and fraud. Different districts of France began to issue their own assignats in small denominations, and this action stirred the National Assembly to evade the solemn pledge that the circulation should not go above twelve hundred millions and that all assignats returned to the treasury for lands should immediately be burned.[23] Within a short time there had been received into the treasury for lands one hundred sixty million livres in paper. By the terms of the previous acts this amount of paper ought to have been retired. Instead of this, under the plea of necessity, the greater part of it was reissued in the form of small notes.

There was, indeed, much excuse for new issues of small notes, for, under the theory that an issue of smaller notes would drive silver out of circulation, the smallest authorized assignat was for fifty livres. To supply silver and copper and hold it in circulation everything was tried. Citizens had been spurred on by law to send their silverware and jewels to the mint. Even the King sent his silver and gold plate, and the churches and convents were required by law to send to the government melting pot all silver and gold vessels not absolutely necessary for public worship. For copper money the church bells were melted down. But silver and even copper continued to become more and more scarce. In the midst of all this, various juggleries were tried, and in November 1790, the Assembly decreed a single standard of coinage, the chosen metal being silver, and the ratio between the two precious metals was changed from $15\frac{1}{2}$ to 1, to $14\frac{1}{2}$ to 1 – but all in vain. It was found necessary to issue the dreaded small paper, and a beginning was made by issuing one hundred millions in notes of five francs, and ere long, obedient to the universal clamour, there were issued parchment notes for various small amounts down to a single sou.[24]

Yet each of these issues, great or small, was but as a drop of cold water to a parched throat. Although there was already a rise in prices which showed that the amount needed for circulation had been exceeded, the cry for 'more circulating medium' was continued. The pressure for new issues became stronger and stronger. The Parisian populace and the Jacobin Club were especially loud in their demands for them; and, a few months later, on June 19, 1791, with few speeches, in a silence very ominous, a new issue was made of six hundred millions more – less than nine months after the former great issue, with its solemn pledges to keep down the amount in circulation. With the exception of a few thoughtful men, the whole nation again sang paeans.[25]

In this comparative ease of new issues is seen the action of a law in finance as certain as the working of a similar law in natural philosophy. If a material body falls from a height its velocity is accelerated, by a well-known law, in a constantly increasing ratio: so in issues of irredeemable currency, in obedience to the theories of a legislative body or of the people at large, there is a natural law of rapidly increasing emission and depreciation. The first inflation bills were passed with great difficulty, after very sturdy resistance and by a majority of a few score out of nearly a thousand votes; but we observe now that new inflation measures were passed more and more easily, and we shall have occasion to see the working of this same law in a more striking degree as this history develops itself.

During the various stages of this debate there cropped up a doctrine old and ominous. It was the same which appeared toward the end of the nineteenth century in the United States during what became known as the 'greenback craze' and the free 'silver craze.' In France it had been refuted, a generation before the Revolution, by Turgot, just as brilliantly as it was met a hundred years later in the United States by James A. Garfield and his compeers. This was the doctrine that all currency, whether gold, paper, leather, or any other material, derives its efficiency from the official stamp it bears, and that, this being the case, a government may relieve itself of all its debts and make itself rich and prosperous simply by means of a printing press – fundamentally the theory which underlay the later American doctrine of 'fiat money.'

There came mutterings and finally speeches in the Jacobin Club, in the Assembly, and in newspaper articles and pamphlets throughout the country, taking this doctrine for granted. These could hardly affect thinking men who bore in mind the calamities brought upon the whole people, and especially upon the poorer classes, by this same theory as put in practice by John Law, or as refuted by Turgot, but it served to swell the popular chorus in favour of the issue of more assignats and plenty of them.[26]

The great majority of Frenchmen now became desperate optimists, declaring that inflation is prosperity. Throughout France there came temporary good feeling. The nation was becoming inebriated with paper money. The good feeling was that of a drunkard just after his draught; and it is to be noted as a simple historical fact, corresponding to a physiological fact, that, as draughts of paper money came faster the successive periods of good feeling grew shorter.

Various bad signs began to appear. Immediately after each new issue came a marked depreciation; curious it is to note the general reluctance to assign the right reason. The decline in the purchasing power of paper money was in obedience to the simplest laws in economics, but France had now gone beyond her thoughtful statesmen and taken refuge in unwavering optimism, giving any explanation of the new difficulties rather than the right one. A leading member of the Assembly insisted, in an elaborate speech, that the cause of depreciation was simply the want of knowledge and of confidence among the rural population and he suggested means of enlightening them. La Rochefoucauld proposed to issue an address to the people showing the goodness of the currency and the absurdity of preferring coin. The address was unanimously voted. As well might they have attempted to show that a beverage made by mixing a quarter of wine and two quarts of water would possess all the exhilarating quality of the original, undiluted liquid.

Attention was aroused by another menacing fact: specie disappeared more and more. The explanations of this fact also displayed wonderful ingenuity in finding false reasons and in evading the true one. A very common explanation was indicated in Prudhomme's newspaper, *Les Révolutions de Paris*, of January 17, 1791, which declared that coin 'will keep rising until the people shall have hanged a broker.' Another popular theory was that the Bourbon family were, in some mysterious way, drawing off all solid money to the chief centres of their intrigues in Germany. Comic and, at the same time, pathetic, were evidences of the widespread idea that if only a goodly number of people engaged in trade were hanged, the par value of the assignats would be restored.

Still another favourite idea was that British emissaries were in the midst of the people, instilling notions hostile to paper. Great efforts were made to find these emissaries and more than one innocent person experienced the popular wrath under the supposition that he was engaged in raising gold and depressing paper. Even Talleyrand, shrewd as he was, insisted that the cause was simply that the imports were too great and the exports too little.[27] As well might he explain the fact that, when oil is mingled with water, water sinks to the bottom, by saying that this is because the oil rises to the top. This disappearance of specie was the result of a natural law as simple and as sure in its action as gravitation; the superior currency had been withdrawn because an inferior currency could be used.[28] Some efforts were made to remedy this. In the municipality of Quilleboeuf a considerable amount in specie having been found in the possession of a citizen, the money was seized and sent to the Assembly. The people of that town treated this hoarded gold as the result of unpatriotic wickedness or madness, instead of seeing that it was but the sure result of a law working in every land and time when certain causes are present.

Marat followed out this theory by asserting that death was the proper penalty for persons who thus hid their money.

Still another troublesome fact began now to appear. Though paper money had increased in amount, prosperity had steadily diminished. In spite of all the paper issues, commercial activity grew more and more spasmodic. Enterprise was chilled and business became more and more stagnant. Mirabeau, in his speech which decided the second great issue of paper, had insisted that, though bankers might suffer, this issue would be of great service to manufacturers and restore prosperity to them and their workmen. The latter were for a time deluded, but were at last rudely awakened from this delusion. The plenty of currency had at first stimulated production and created a great activity in manufactures, but soon the markets were glutted and the demand was diminished.

In spite of the wretched financial policy of years gone by, and especially in spite of the Revocation of the Edict of Nantes, by which religious bigotry had driven out of the kingdom thousands of its most skilful Protestant workmen, the manufactures of France had before the Revolution come into full bloom. In the finer woollen goods, in silk and satin fabrics of all sorts, in choice pottery and porcelain, in manufactures of iron, steel, and copper, they had again taken their old leading place upon the Continent. All the previous changes had, at the worst, done no more than to inflict a momentary check on this highly developed system of manufactures. But what the bigotry of Louis XIV and the shiftlessness of Louis XV could not do in nearly a century, was accomplished by this tampering with the currency in a few months. One manufactory after another stopped. At one town, Lodève, five thousand workmen were discharged from the cloth manufactories. Every cause except the right one was assigned for this. Heavy duties were put upon foreign goods; everything that tariffs and customhouses could do was done. Still the great manufactories of Normandy were closed, those of the rest of the kingdom speedily followed, and vast numbers of workmen in all parts of the country were thrown out of employment.[29] Nor was this the case with the home demand alone. The foreign demand which at first had been stimulated, soon fell off.

In no way can this be better stated than by one of the most thoughtful historians of modern times, who says, 'It is true that at first the assignats gave the same impulse to business in the city as in the country, but the apparent improvement had no firm foundation, even in the towns. Whenever a great quantity of paper money is suddenly issued we invariably see a rapid increase of trade. The great quantity of the circulating medium sets in motion all the energies of commerce and manufactures; capital for investment is more easily found than usual and trade perpetually receives fresh nutriment. If this paper represents real credit, founded upon order and legal security, from which it can derive a firm and lasting value, such a movement may be the starting point of a great and widely-extended prosperity, as, for instance, a splendid improvement in English agriculture was undoubtedly owing to the emancipation of the country bankers. If on the contrary, the new paper is of precarious value, as was clearly seen to be the case with the French assignats as early as February 1791, it can confer no lasting benefits. For the moment, perhaps, business receives an impulse, all the more violent because everyone endeavours to invest his doubtful paper in buildings, machines, and goods, which, under all circumstances, retain some intrinsic value. Such a movement was witnessed in France in 1791, and from every quarter there came satisfactory reports of the activity of manufactures.

'But, for the moment, the French manufacturers derived great advantage from this state of things. As their products could be so cheaply paid for, orders poured in from foreign countries to such a degree that it was often difficult for the manufacturers to satisfy their customers. It is easy to see that prosperity of this kind must very soon find its limit. ... When a further fall in the assignats took place, this prosperity would necessarily collapse and be succeeded by a crisis all the more destructive the more deeply men had engaged in speculation under the influence of the first favourable prospects.'[30]

Thus came a collapse in manufacturing and commerce, just as it had come previously in France: just as it came at various periods in Austria, Russia, America, and in all countries where men have tried to build up prosperity on irredeemable paper.[31]

All this breaking down of the manufactures and commerce of the nation made fearful inroads on the greater fortunes; but upon the lesser, and upon the little properties of the masses of the nation who relied upon their labour, it pressed with intense severity. The capitalist could put his surplus paper money into the government lands and await results; but the men who needed their money from day to day suffered the worst of the misery.

Still another difficulty appeared. There had come a complete uncertainty as to the future. Long before the close of 1791 no one knew whether a piece of paper money representing a hundred livres would, a month later, have a purchasing power of ninety or eighty or sixty livres. The result was that capitalists feared to embark their means in business. Enterprise received a mortal blow. Demand for labour was still further diminished; and here came a new cause for calamity, for this uncertainty withered all far-reaching undertakings. The business of France dwindled into a mere living from hand to mouth.

This state of things, too, while it bore heavily upon the moneyed classes, was still more ruinous to those in moderate and, most of all, to those in straitened circumstances. With the masses of the people, the purchase of every article of supply became a speculation – a speculation in which the professional speculator had an immense advantage over the ordinary buyer. Says the most brilliant of apologists for French revolutionary statesmanship, 'Commerce was dead; betting took its place.'[32]

Nor was there any compensating advantage to the mercantile class. The merchant was forced to add to his ordinary profit a sum sufficient to cover probable or possible fluctuations in value; and while prices of products thus went higher, the wages of labour, owing to the number of workmen who were thrown out of employment, went lower.

But these evils, though great, were small compared to those far more deep-seated signs of disease which now showed themselves throughout the country. One of these was the *obliteration of thrift* from the minds of the French people. The French are naturally thrifty; but, with such masses of money and with such uncertainty as to its future value, the ordinary motives for saving and care diminished, and a loose luxury spread throughout the country.

A still worse outgrowth was the increase of speculation and gambling. With the plethora of paper currency in 1791 appeared the first evidences of that cancerous disease which always follows large issues of irredeemable currency – a disease more permanently injurious to a nation than war, pestilence, or famine. For at the great metropolitan centres grew a luxurious, speculative stock-gambling body, which, like a malignant tumor, absorbed into itself the strength of the nation and sent out its cancerous fibres to the remotest hamlets. At these city centres abundant wealth seemed to be piled up. In the country at large there grew a dislike of steady labour and a contempt for moderate gains and simple living.

In a pamphlet published in May 1791, we see how, in regard to this also, public opinion was blinded. The author calls attention to the increase of gambling in values of all sorts in these words: 'What shall I say of the stockjobbing, as frightful as it is scandalous, which goes on in Paris under the very eyes of our legislators – a most terrible evil, yet, under the present circumstances, necessary?' The author also speaks of these stock gamblers as using the most insidious means to influence public opinion in favour of their measures; and then proposes, seriously, a change in various matters of detail, thinking that this would prove a sufficient remedy for an evil which had its roots far down in the whole system of irredeemable currency. As well might a physician prescribe a pimple wash for a diseased liver.[33]

Now began to be seen more plainly some of the many ways in which an inflation policy robs the working class. As these knots of plotting schemers at the city centres were becoming bloated with sudden wealth, the producing classes of the country, though having in their possession more and more currency, grew lean. In the schemes and speculations put forth by stockjobbers and stimulated by the printing of more currency, multitudes of small fortunes were absorbed and lost while a few swollen fortunes were rapidly aggregated in the larger cities. This crippled a large class in the country districts, which had employed a great number of workmen.

In the leading French cities now arose a luxury and license which was a greater evil even than the plundering which ministered to it. In the country the gambling spirit spread more and more. Says the same thoughtful historian whom I have already quoted: 'What a prospect for a country when its rural population was changed into a great band of gamblers!'[34]

Nor was this reckless and corrupt spirit confined to businessmen; it began to break out in official circles, and public men who, a few years before, had been thought above all possibility of taint, became luxurious, reckless, cynical, and finally corrupt. Mirabeau himself, who, not many months previous, had risked imprisonment and even death to establish constitutional government, was now – at this very time – secretly receiving heavy bribes. When, at the downfall of the monarchy a few years later, the famous iron chest of the Tuileries was opened, there were found evidences that, in this carnival of inflation and corruption, he had been a regularly paid servant of the Royal court.[35]

The artful plundering of the people at large was bad enough, but worse still was this growing corruption in official and legislative circles. Out of the speculating and gambling of the inflation period grew luxury, and, out of this, corruption. It grew as naturally as a fungus on a muck heap. It was first felt in business operations, but soon began to be seen in the legislative body and in journalism. Mirabeau was, by no means, the only example. Such members of the legislative body as Jullien of Toulouse, Delaunay of Angers, Fabre d'Eglantine, and their disciples, were among the most noxious of those conspiring by legislative action to raise and depress securities for stockjobbing purposes. Bribery of legislators followed as a matter of course. Delaunay, Jullien, and Chabot accepted a bribe of five hundred thousand livres for aiding legislation calculated to promote the purposes of certain stockjobbers. It is some comfort to know that nearly all concerned were guillotined for it.[36]

It is true that the number of these corrupt legislators was small, far less than alarmists led the nation to suppose, but there were enough to cause widespread distrust, cynicism, and want of faith in any patriotism or any virtue.

What It Brought

Even worse than this was the breaking down of the morals of the country at large, resulting from the sudden building up of ostentatious wealth in a few large cities, and from the gambling, speculative spirit spreading from these to the small towns and rural districts. From this was developed an even more disgraceful result – the decay of a true sense of national good faith. The patriotism which the fear of the absolute monarchy, the machinations of the court party, the menaces of the army, and the threats of all monarchical Europe had been unable to shake was gradually disintegrated by this same speculative, stockjobbing habit fostered by the superabundant currency.

At the outset, in the discussions preliminary to the first issue of paper money, Mirabeau and others who had favoured it had insisted that patriotism, as well as an enlightened self-interest, would lead the people to keep up the value of paper money. The very opposite of this was now revealed, for there appeared, as another outgrowth of this disease, what has always been seen under similar circumstances. It is a result of previous and a cause of future evils. This outgrowth was a vast debtor class in the nation, directly interested in the depreciation of the currency in which they were to pay their debts. The nucleus of this class was formed by those who had purchased the church lands from the government. Only small payments down had been required and the remainder was to be paid in deferred installments. An indebtedness of a multitude of people had thus been created to the amount of hundreds of millions.

This body of debtors soon saw, of course, that their interest was to depreciate the currency in which their debts were to be paid; and these were speedily joined by a far more influential class – by that class whose speculative tendencies had been stimulated by the abundance of paper money, and who had gone largely into debt, looking for a rise in nominal values. Soon demagogues of the viler sort in the political clubs began to pander to it; a little later important persons in this debtor class were to be found intriguing in the Assembly – first in its seats and later in more conspicuous places of public trust. Before long, the debtor class became a powerful body extending through all ranks of society. From the stock gambler who sat in the Assembly to the small land speculator in the rural districts; from the sleek inventor of canards on the Paris Exchange to the lying stockjobber in the market town, all pressed vigorously for new issues of paper; all were apparently able to demonstrate to the people that in new issues of paper lay the only chance for national prosperity.

This great debtor class, relying on the multitude who could be approached by superficial arguments, soon gained control. Strange as it might seem to those who have not watched the same causes at work at a previous period in France and at various times in other countries, while every issue of paper money really made matters worse, a superstition gained ground among the people at large that, if only *enough* paper money were issued and were more cunningly handled, the poor would be made rich. Henceforth, all opposition was futile. In December 1791, a report was made in the Legislative Assembly in favour of yet another great issue of three hundred millions more of paper money. In regard to this report Cambon said that more money was needed but asked, 'Will you, in a moment when stockjobbing is carried on with such fury, give it new power by adding so much more to the circulation?' But such high considerations were now little regarded. Dorisy declared, 'There is not enough money yet in circulation; if there were more, the sales of national lands would be more rapid.' And the official report of his speech states that these words were applauded.

Dorisy then went on to insist that the government lands were worth at least thirty-five hundred million livres and said: 'Why should members ascend the tribunal and disquiet France? Fear nothing; your currency reposes upon a sound mortgage.' Then followed a glorification of the patriotism of the French people, which, he asserted, would carry the nation through all its difficulties.

Becquet, speaking next, declared that 'the circulation is becoming more rare every day.'

On December 17, 1791, a new issue was ordered, making in all twenty-one hundred millions authorized. Coupled with this was the declaration that the total amount in actual circulation should never reach more than sixteen hundred millions. Before this issue the value of the 100 livres note had fallen at Paris to about 80 livres;[37] immediately afterward it fell to about 68 livres. What limitations of the currency were worth may be judged from the fact that not only had the declaration made hardly a year before, limiting the amount in circulation to twelve hundred millions, been violated, but the declaration, made hardly a month previous, in which the Assembly had as solemnly limited the amount of circulation to fourteen hundred millions, had also been repudiated.

The evils which we have already seen arising from the earlier issues were now aggravated; but the most curious thing evolved out of all this chaos was a *new system of political economy.* In speeches, newspapers, and pamphlets about this time, we begin to find it declared that, after all, a depreciated currency is a blessing; that gold and silver form an unsatisfactory standard for measuring values; that it is a good thing to have a currency that will not go out of the kingdom and which separates France from other nations; that thus shall manufacturers be encouraged; that commerce with other nations may be a curse, and hindrance thereto may be a blessing; that the laws of political economy, however applicable in other times, are not applicable to this particular period, and, however operative in other nations, are not now so in France; that the ordinary rules of political economy are perhaps suited to the minions of despotism but not to the free and enlightened inhabitants of France at the close of the eighteenth century; that the whole state of present things, so far from being an evil, is a blessing. All these ideas, and others quite as striking, were brought to the surface in the debates on the various new issues.[38]

Within four months came another report to the Assembly as ingenious as those preceding. It declared: 'Your committee are thoroughly persuaded that the amount of the circulating medium before the Revolution was greater than that of the assignats today: but at that time the money circulated slowly and now it passes rapidly so that one thousand million assignats do the work of two thousand millions of specie.' The report foretells further increase in prices, but by some curious jugglery reaches a conclusion favourable to further inflation. Despite these encouragements the assignats nominally worth 100 livres had fallen, at the beginning of February 1792, to about 60 livres, and during that month fell to 53 lives.[39]

In March, Clavière became Minister of Finance. He was especially proud of his share in the invention and advocacy of the assignats, and now pressed their creation more vigorously than ever; and on April 30, of the same year, came the fifth great issue of paper money, amounting to three hundred millions. At about the same time Cambon sneered ominously at public creditors as 'rich people, old financiers, and bankers.' Soon payment was suspended on dues to public creditors for all amounts exceeding ten thousand francs.

This was hailed by many as a measure in the interests of the poorer classes of people, but the result was that it injured them most of all. Henceforward, until the end of this history, capital was quietly taken from labour and locked up in all the ways that financial ingenuity could devise. All that saved thousands of labourers in France from starvation was that they were drafted off into the army and sent to be killed on foreign battlefields.

On the last day of July 1792, came another brilliant report from Fouquet, showing that the total amount of currency already issued was about twenty-four hundred millions, but claiming that the national lands were worth a little more than this sum. A decree was now passed issuing three hundred millions more. By this the prices of everything were again enhanced save one thing, and that one thing was *labour*. Strange as it may at first appear, while the depreciation of the currency had raised all products enormously in price, the stoppage of so many manufactories and the withdrawal of capital caused wages in the summer of 1792, after all the inflation, to be as small as they had been four years before – viz., fifteen sous per day. No more striking example can be seen of the truth uttered by Daniel Webster, that 'of all the contrivances for cheating the labouring classes of mankind, none has been more effective than that which deludes them with paper money.'[40]

Issue after issue followed at intervals of a few months, until, on December 14, 1792, we have an official statement to the effect that thirty-four hundred millions had been put forth, of which six hundred millions had been burned, leaving in circulation twenty-eight hundred millions.

When it is remembered that there was little business to do and that the purchasing power of the livre or franc, when judged by the staple products of the country, was equal to about half the present purchasing power of our own dollar, it will be seen into what evils France had drifted. As the mania for paper money ran its course, even the sous, obtained by melting down the church bells, were more and more driven out of circulation and more and more parchment notes from twenty sous to five were issued, and at last pieces of one sou, of half a sou, and even of one-quarter of a sou were put in circulation.[41]

But now another source of wealth was opened to the nation. There came a confiscation of the large estates of landed proprietors who had fled the country. An estimate in 1793 made the value of these estates three billions of francs. As a consequence, the issues of paper money were continued in increased amounts, on the old theory that they were guaranteed by the solemn pledge of these lands belonging to the state. Under the Legislative Assembly through the year 1792, new issues were made virtually every month, so that at the end of January 1793, it was more and more realized that the paper money actually in circulation amounted close upon three thousand millions of francs. All this had been issued publicly, in open sessions of the National and Legislative Assemblies; but now under the National Convention, the two Committees of Public Safety and of Finance began to decree new issues privately, in secret session.

As a result, the issues became larger still, and four hundred workmen were added to those previously engaged in furnishing this paper money, and these were so pressed with work from six o'clock in the morning until eight in the evening that they struck for higher wages and were successful.[42]

The consequences of these overissues now began to be more

painfully evident to the people at large. Articles of common consumption became enormously dear and prices were constantly rising. Orators in the Legislative Assembly, clubs, local meetings, and elsewhere now endeavoured to enlighten people by assigning every reason for this depreciation save the true one. They declaimed against the corruption of the ministry, the want of patriotism among the Moderates, the intrigues of the emigrant nobles, the hard-heartedness of the rich, the monopolizing spirit of the merchants, the perversity of the shopkeepers – each and all of these as causes of the difficulty.[43]

This decline in the government paper was at first somewhat masked by fluctuations. For at various times the value of the currency *rose*. The victory of Jemappes and the general success of the French army against the invaders, with the additional security offered by new confiscations of land, caused, in November 1792, an appreciation in the value of the currency; the franc had stood at 57 and it rose to about 69; but the downward tendency was soon resumed and in September 1793, the assignats had sunk below 30. Then sundry new victories and coruscations of oratory gave momentary confidence so that in December 1793, they rose above 50. But despite these fluctuations the downward tendency soon became more rapid than ever.[44]

The washerwomen of Paris, finding soap so dear that they could hardly purchase it, insisted that all the merchants who were endeavouring to save something of their little property by refusing to sell their goods for the wretched currency with which France was flooded, should be punished with death; the women of the markets and the hangers-on of the Jacobin Club called loudly for a law 'to equalize the value of paper money and silver coin.' It was also demanded that a tax be laid especially on the rich, to the amount of four hundred million francs, to buy bread. Marat declared loudly that the people, by hanging shopkeepers and plundering stores, could easily remove the trouble.

The result was that on February 28, 1793, at eight o'clock in the evening, a mob of men and women in disguise began plundering the stores and shops of Paris. At first they demanded only bread; soon they insisted on coffee and rice and sugar; at last they seized everything on which they could lay their hands – cloth, clothing, groceries, and luxuries of every kind. Two hundred such places were plundered. This was endured for six hours, and finally order was restored only by a grant of seven million francs to buy off the mob. The new political economy was beginning to bear its fruits luxuriantly. A gaudy growth of it appeared at the City Hall of Paris when, in response to the complaints of the plundered merchants, Roux declared, in the midst of great applause, that 'shopkeepers were only giving back to the people what they had hitherto robbed them of'.

The mob having thus been bought off by concessions and appeased by oratory, the government gained time to think, and now came a series of amazing expedients – and yet all perfectly logical.

Three of these have gained in French history an evil pre-eminence, and first of the three was the Forced Loan.

In view of the fact that the well-to-do citizens were thought to be lukewarm in their support of the politicians controlling the country, various demagogues in the National Convention, which had now succeeded the National, Constituent, and Legislative Assemblies, found ample matter for denunciations long and loud. The result outside the Convention was increased activity of the guillotine. The results inside were new measures against all who had money, and on June 22, 1793, the Convention determined that there should be a Forced Loan, secured on the confiscated lands of the emigrants and levied upon all married men with incomes of ten thousand francs, and upon all unmarried men with incomes of six thousand francs. It was calculated that these would bring into the treasury a thousand millions of francs.

But a difficulty was found. So many of the rich had fled or had concealed their wealth that only a fifth of the sum required could be raised, and therefore a law was soon passed which levied forced loans upon incomes as low as one thousand francs – or, say, two hundred dollars of American money. This tax was made progressive. On the smaller proprietors it was fixed at one-tenth and on the larger, that is, on all incomes above nine thousand francs, it was made one-half of the entire income. Little, if any, provision was made for the repayment of this loan but the certificates might be used for purchasing the confiscated real estate of the church and of the nobility.[45]

But if this first expedient shows how naturally a 'fiat' money system runs into despotism, the next is no less instructive in showing how easily it becomes repudiation and dishonour.

As we have seen, the first issue of the assignats – made by the

National Assembly – bore a portrait of the King; but on the various issues after the establishment of a republic this emblem had been discarded. This change led to a difference in value between the earlier and the later paper money. The wild follies of fanatics and demagogues had led to an increasing belief that the existing state of things could not last; that the Bourbons must ere long return; that in such case, while a new monarch would repudiate all the vast mass of the later paper issued by the Republic, he would recognize that first issue bearing the face and therefore the guarantee of the King. So it was that this first issue came to bear a higher value than those of later date.

To meet this condition of things it was now proposed to repudiate all that earlier issue. In vain did sundry more thoughtful members of the Convention plead that this paper money, amounting to five hundred fifty-eight millions of francs, bore the solemn guarantee of the nation, as well as of the King; the current was irresistible. All that Cambon, the great leader of finance at that time, could secure was a clause claiming to protect the poor, to the effect that this demonetization should not extend to notes below a hundred francs in value; and it was also agreed that any of the notes, large or small, might be received in payment of taxes and for the confiscated property of the clergy and nobility. To all the arguments advanced against this breach of the national faith Danton, then at the height of his power, simply declared that only aristocrats could favour notes bearing the royal portrait, and gave forth his famous utterance: 'Imitate Nature, which watches over the preservation of the race but has no regard for individuals'. The decree was passed on July 31, 1793, yet its futility was apparent in less than two months, when the Convention decreed that there should be issued two thousand millions of francs more in assignats between the values of ten sous and four hundred francs, and when, before the end of the year, five hundred millions more were authorized.[46]

The third outgrowth of the vast issue of fiat money was the 'Maximum'. As far back as November 1792, the Terrorist associate of Robespierre, St. Just, in view of the steady rise in prices of the necessaries of life, had proposed a scheme by which these prices should be established by law, at a rate proportionate to the wages of the working classes. This plan lingered in men's minds, taking shape in various resolutions and decrees until the whole culminated on

September 29, 1793, in the Law of the Maximum.

While all this legislation was highhanded, it was not careless. Even statesmen of the greatest strength, having once been drawn into this flood, were borne on into excesses which, a little earlier, would have appalled them. Committees of experts were appointed to study the whole subject of prices, and at last there were adopted the great 'four rules' which seemed to statesmen of that time a masterly solution of the whole difficulty.[47]

First, the price of each article of necessity was to be fixed at one and one-third its price in 1790. *Secondly*, all transportation was to be added at a fixed rate per league. *Thirdly*, five per cent was to be added for the profit of the wholesaler. *Fourthly*, ten per cent was to be added for the profit of the retailer. Nothing could look more reasonable. Great was the jubilation. The report was presented and supported by Barrère – 'the tiger monkey' – then in all the glory of his great orations: now best known from his portrait by Macaulay. Nothing could withstand Barrère's eloquence. He insisted that France had been suffering from a '*Monarchical* commerce which only sought wealth', while what she needed and what she was now to receive was a '*Republican* commerce – a commerce of moderate profits and virtuous'. He exulted in the fact that 'France alone enjoys such a commerce – that it exists in no other nation'. He poured contempt over political economy as 'that science which quacks have corrupted, which pedants have obscured, and which academicians have depreciated'. France, he said, has something better, and he declared in conclusion, 'The needs of the people will no longer be spied upon in order that the commercial classes may arbitrarily take advantage.'[48]

The first result of the Maximum was that every means was taken to evade the fixed price imposed, and the farmers brought in as little produce as they possibly could. This increased the scarcity, and the people of the large cities were put on an allowance. Tickets were issued authorizing the bearer to obtain at the official prices a certain amount of bread or sugar or soap or wood or coal to cover immediate necessities.[49]

But it was found that the Maximum, with its divinely revealed four rules, could not be made to work well – even by the shrewdest devices. In the greater part of France it could not be enforced. As to merchandise of foreign origin or merchandise into which any foreign product entered, the war had raised it far above the price allowed under the first rule, namely, the price of 1790 with an addition of one-third. Shopkeepers therefore could not sell such goods without ruin. The result was that very many went out of business, and the remainder forced buyers to pay enormous charges under the very natural excuse that the seller risked his life in trading at all. That this excuse was valid is easily seen by the daily lists of those condemned to the guillotine, in which not infrequently figure the names of men charged with violating the Maximum laws. Manufactures were very generally crippled and frequently destroyed, and agriculture was fearfully depressed. To detect goods concealed by farmers and shopkeepers, a spy system was established with a reward to the informer of one-third of the value of the goods discovered. To spread terror, the Criminal Tribunal at Strassburg was ordered to destroy the dwelling of anyone found guilty of selling goods above the price set by law. The farmer often found that he could not raise his products at anything like the price required by the new law; and when he tried to hold back his crops or cattle, alleging that he could not afford to sell them at the prices fixed by law, they were frequently taken from him by force and he was fortunate if paid even in the depreciated fiat money – fortunate, indeed, if he finally escaped with his life.[50]

Involved in all these perplexities, the Convention tried to cut the Gordian knot. It decreed that any person selling gold or silver coin, or making any difference in any transaction between paper and specie, should be imprisoned in irons for six years; that anyone who refused to accept a payment in assignats, or accepted assignats at a discount, should pay a fine of three thousand francs; and that anyone committing this crime a second time should pay a fine of six thousand francs and suffer imprisonment twenty years in irons. Later, on September 8, 1793, the penalty for such offenses was made death, with confiscation of the criminal's property, and a reward was offered to any person informing the authorities regarding any such criminal transaction. To reach the climax of ferocity, the Convention decreed, in May 1794, that the death penalty should be inflicted on any person convicted of 'having asked, before a bargain was concluded, in what money payment was to be made.' Nor was this all. The great finance minister, Cambon, soon saw that the worst enemies of his policy were gold and silver. Therefore it was that, under his lead, the Convention closed the Exchange and finally, on November 13, 1793, under terrifying penalties, suppressed all commerce in the precious metals. About a year later came the abolition of the Maximum itself.[51]

It is easily seen that these Maximum laws were perfectly logical. Whenever any nation intrusts to its legislators the issue of a currency not based on the idea of redemption in standard coin recognized in the commerce of civilized nations, it intrusts to them the power to raise or depress the value of every article in the possession of every citizen. Louis XIV had claimed that all property in France was his own, and that what private persons held was as much his as if it were in his coffers. But even this assumption is exceeded by the confiscating power exercised in a country, where, instead of leaving values to be measured by a standard common to the whole world, they are left to be depressed or raised at the whim, caprice, or interest of a body of legislators. When this power is given, the power of fixing prices is inevitably included in it.[52]

It may be said that these measures were made necessary by the war then going on. Nothing could be more baseless than such an objection. In this war the French soon became generally successful. It was quickly pushed mainly upon foreign soil. Numerous contributions were levied upon the subjugated countries to support the French armies. The war was one of those in which the loss, falling apparently on future generations, first stimulates, in a sad way, trade and production. The main cause of these evils was tampering with the circulating medium of an entire nation; keeping all values in fluctuation; discouraging enterprise; paralyzing energy; undermining sobriety; obliterating thrift; promoting extravagance; and exciting riot by the issue of an irredeemable currency. The true business way of meeting the enormous demands on France during the first years of the Revolution had been stated by a true statesman and sound financier, Du Pont de Nemours, at the very beginning. He had shown that using the same paper as a circulating medium and as a means for selling the national real estate was like using the same implement for an oyster knife and a razor.[53]

It has been argued that the assignats sank in value because they were not well secured – that securing them on government real estate was as futile as if the United States had, in the financial troubles of its early days, secured notes on its real estate. This objection is utterly fallacious. The government lands of our country were remote from the centres of capital and difficult to examine; the French national real estate was near these centres – even *in* them – and easy to examine. Our national real estate was unimproved and unproductive; theirs was improved and productive, its average productiveness in market in ordinary times being from four to five per cent.[54]

It has also been objected that the attempt to secure the assignats on government real estate failed because of the general want of confidence in the title derived by the purchasers from the new government. Every thorough student of that period must know that this is a misleading statement. Everything shows that the vast majority of the French people had a fanatical confidence in the stability of the new government during the greater part of the Revolution. There were disbelievers in the security of the assignats just as there were disbelievers in the paper money of the United States throughout our Civil War; but they were usually a small minority. Even granting that there was a doubt as to investment in French lands, the French people certainly had as much confidence in the secure possession of government lands as any people can ever have in large issues of government bonds. Indeed, it is certain that they had far more confidence in their lands as a security than modern nations can usually have in large issues of bonds obtained by payments of irredeemable paper. One simple fact, as stated by John Stuart Mill, which made assignats difficult to convert into real estate, was that the vast majority of people could not afford to make investments outside their business; and this fact is no less fatal to any attempt to contract large issues of irredeemable paper – save, perhaps, a bold, statesmanlike attempt which seizes the best time and presses every advantage, eschewing all juggling devices and sacrificing everything to maintain a sound currency based on standards common to the entire financial world.

And now was seen, taking possession of the nation, that idea which developed so easily out of the fiat money system – the idea that the ordinary needs of government may be legitimately met wholly by the means of paper currency; that taxes may be dispensed with. As a result, it was found that the assignat printing press was the one resource left to the government, and the increase in the volume of paper money became every day more appalling.

It will doubtless surprise many to learn that, in spite of these evident results of too much currency, the old cry of a 'scarcity of circulating medium' was not stilled; it appeared not long after each issue, no matter how large.

But every thoughtful student of financial history knows that this cry always comes after such issues – nay, that it *must* come – because in obedience to a natural law, the former scarcity, or rather *insufficiency* of currency, recurs just as soon as prices become adjusted to the new volume, and there comes some little revival of business with the usual increase of credit.[55]

In August 1793, appeared a new report by Cambon. No one can read it without being struck by its mingled ability and folly. His final plan of dealing with the public debt has outlasted all revolutions since, but his disposition of the inflated currency came to a wretched failure. Against Du Pont, who showed conclusively that the wild increase of paper money was leading straight to ruin, Cambon carried the majority in the great assemblies and clubs by sheer audacity – the audacity of desperation. Zeal in supporting the assignats became his religion. The National Convention which succeeded the Legislative Assembly, issued in 1793 over three thousand millions of assignats, and, of these, over twelve hundred millions were poured into the circulation. And yet Cambon steadily insisted that the security for the assignat currency was perfect. The climax of his zeal was reached when he counted as assets in the national treasury the indemnities which, he declared, France was sure to receive after future victories over the allied nations with which she was then waging a desperate war. As patriotism it was sublime; as finance it was deadly.[56]

Everything was tried. Very elaborately he devised a funding scheme which, taken in connection with his system of issues, was in effect what in these days would be called an 'interconvertibility scheme.' By various degrees of persuasion or force – the guillotine looming up in the background – holders of assignats were urged to convert them into evidence of national debt, bearing interest at five per cent, with the understanding that if more paper were afterward needed more would be issued. All in vain. The official tables of depreciation show that the assignats continued to fall. A forced loan, calling in a billion of these, checked this fall, but only for a moment. The 'interconvertibility scheme' between currency and bonds failed as dismally as the 'interconvertibility scheme' between currency and land had failed.[57]

A more effective expedient was a law confiscating the property of all Frenchmen who left France after July 14, 1789, and who had not returned. This gave new land to be mortgaged for the security of paper money.

All this vast chapter in financial folly is sometimes referred to as if it resulted from the direct action of men utterly unskilled in finance. This is a grave error. That wild schemers and dreamers took a leading part in setting the fiat money system going is true; that speculation and interested financiers made it worse is also true; but the men who had charge of French finance during the Reign of Terror and who made these experiments, which seem to us so monstrous, in order to rescue themselves and their country from the flood which was sweeping everything to financial ruin were universally recognized as among the most skilful and honest financiers in Europe. Cambon, especially, ranked then and ranks now as among the most expert in any period. The disastrous results of all his courage and ability in the attempt to stand against the deluge of paper money show how powerless are the most skilful masters of finance to stem the tide of fiat money calamity when once it is fairly under headway; and how useless are all enactments which they can devise against the underlying laws of nature.

Month after month, year after year, new issues went on. Meanwhile, everything possible was done to keep up the value of paper. The city authorities of Metz took a solemn oath that the assignats should bear the same price whether in paper or specie, and whether in buying or selling, and various other official bodies throughout the nation followed this example. In obedience to those who believed with the market women of Paris, as stated in their famous petition, that 'laws should be passed making paper money as good as gold', Couthon, in August 1793, had proposed and carried a law punishing any person who should sell assignats at less than their nominal value with imprisonment for twenty years in chains, and later carried a law making investments in foreign countries by Frenchmen punishable with death.[58]

But to the surprise of the great majority of the French people, the value of the assignats was found, after the momentary spasm of fear had passed, not to have been permanently increased by these measures. On the contrary, this 'fiat' paper persisted in obeying the natural laws of finance and, as new issues increased, their value decreased. Nor did the most lavish aid of nature avail. The paper money of the nation seemed to possess a magic power to transmute prosperity into adversity and plenty into famine. The year 1794 was exceptionally fruitful, and yet with the autumn came scarcity of provisions and with the winter came distress.

The reason is perfectly simple. The sequences in that whole history are absolutely logical. First, the Assembly had inflated the currency and raised prices enormously. Next, it had been forced to establish an arbitrary maximum price for produce. But this price, large as it seemed, soon fell below the real value of produce; many of the farmers, therefore, raised less produce or refrained from bringing what they had to market.[59] But, as is usual in such cases, the trouble was ascribed to everything rather than the real cause, and the most severe measures were established in all parts of the country to force farmers to bring produce to market, millers to grind, and shopkeepers to sell it.[60]

The issues of paper money continued. Toward the end of 1794 seven thousand millions in assignats were in circulation.[61] By the end of May 1795, the circulation was increased to ten thousand millions; at the end of July, to fourteen thousand millions; and the value of one hundred francs in paper fell steadily, first to four francs in gold, then to three, then to two and one-half.[62] But, curiously enough, while this depreciation was rapidly going on, as at various other periods when depreciation was rapid, there came an apparent revival of business. The hopes of many were revived by the fact that in spite of the decline of paper there was an exceedingly brisk trade in all kinds of permanent property. Whatever articles of permanent value certain needy people were willing to sell, certain cunning people were willing to buy and to pay good prices for in assignats.

At this, hope revived for a time in certain quarters. But ere long it was discovered that this was one of the most distressing results of a natural law which is sure to come into play under such circumstances. It was simply a feverish activity caused by the intense desire of a large number of the shrewder class to convert their paper money into anything and everything which they could hold and hoard until the collapse which they foresaw should take place. This very activity in business simply indicated the disease. It was simply legal robbery of the more enthusiastic and trusting by the more coldhearted and keen. It was the 'unloading' of the assignats upon the mass of the people.[63]

Interesting is it to note in the midst of all this the steady action of another simple law in finance. Prisons, guillotines, enactments inflicting twenty years' imprisonment in chains upon persons twice convicted of buying or selling paper money at less than its nominal value, and death upon investors in foreign securities, were powerless. The National Convention, fighting a world in arms and with an armed revolt on its own soil, showed titanic power, but in its struggle to circumvent one simple law of nature its weakness was pitiable. The *louis d' or* stood in the market as a monitor, noting each day with unerring fidelity, the decline in value of the assignat; a monitor not to be bribed, not to be scared. As well might the National Convention try to bribe or scare away the polarity of the mariner's compass. On August 1, 1795, this gold louis of 25 francs was worth in paper, 920 francs; on September 1, 1,200 francs; on November 1, 2,600 francs; on December 1, 3,050 francs. In February 1796, it was worth 7,200 francs or one franc in gold was worth 288 francs in paper. Prices of all commodities went up nearly in proportion.[64]

The writings of this period give curious details. Thibaudeau, in his Memoirs, speaks of sugar as 500 francs a pound, soap, 230 francs, candles, 140 francs. Mercier, in his lifelike pictures of the French metropolis at that period, mentions 600 francs as carriage hire for a single drive, and 6,000 for an entire day. Examples from other sources are such as the following: a measure of flour advanced from two francs in 1790, to 225 francs in 1795; a pair of shoes, from five francs to 200; a hat, from 14 francs to 500; butter, to 560 francs a pound; a turkey, to 900 francs.[65] Everything was enormously inflated in price *except the wages of labour*. As manufacturers had closed, wages had fallen, until all that kept them up seemed to be the fact that so many labourers were drafted off into the army.

From this state of things came grievous wrong and gross fraud. Men who had foreseen these results and had gone into debt were of course jubilant. He who in 1790 had borrowed 10,000 francs could pay his debts in 1796 for about 35 francs. Laws were made to meet these abuses. As far back as 1794 a plan was devised for publishing official 'tables of depreciation' to be used in making equitable settlements of debts, but all such machinery proved futile. On May 18, 1796, a young man complained to the National Convention that his elder brother, who had been acting as administrator of his deceased father's estate, had paid the heirs in assignats, and that he had received scarcely one three-hundredth part of the real value of his share.[66]

To meet cases like this, a law was passed establishing a 'scale of proportion.' Taking as a standard the value of the assignat when there were two billions in circulation, this law declared that, in payment of debts, one-quarter should be added to the amount originally borrowed for every five hundred millions added to the circulation. In obedience to this law a man who borrowed two thousand francs when there were two billions in circulation would have to pay his creditors twenty-five hundred francs when half a billion more were added to the currency, and over thirty-five thousand francs before the emissions of paper reached their final amount. This brought new evils, worse, if possible, than the old.[67]

The question will naturally be asked: *On whom did this vast depreciation mainly fall at last?* When this currency had sunk to about one three-hundredth part of its nominal value and, after that, to nothing, in whose hands was the bulk of it? The answer is simple. I shall give it in the exact words of that thoughtful historian from whom I have already quoted: 'Before the end of the year 1795, the paper money was almost exclusively in the hands of the working classes, employees and men of small means, whose property was not large enough to invest in stores of goods or national lands.[68] Financiers and men of large means were shrewd enough to put as much of their property as possible into objects of permanent value. The working classes had no such foresight or skill or means. On them finally came the great crushing weight of the loss. After the first collapse came up the cries of the starving. Roads and bridges were neglected; many manufactures were given up in utter hopelessness'. To continue, in the words of the historian already cited: 'None felt any confidence in the future in any respect; few dared to make a business investment for any length of time, and it was accounted a folly to curtail the pleasures of the moment, to accumulate or save for sò uncertain a future.'[69]

This system in finance was accompanied by a system in politics no less startling, and each system tended to aggravate the other. The wild radicals, having sent to the guillotine first all the Royalists and next all the leading Republicans they could entrap, the various factions began sending each other to the same destination: Hébertists, Dantonists, with various other factions and groups, and, finally, the Robespierrists, followed each other in rapid succession. After these declaimers and phrase-mongers had thus disappeared, there came to power, in October 1795, a new government – mainly a survival of the more scoundrelly – the

Directory. It found the country utterly impoverished, and its only resource at first was to print more paper and to issue even while wet from the press. These new issues were made at last by the two great committees, with or without warrant of law, and in greater sums than ever. Complaints were made that the army of engravers and printers at the mint could not meet the demand for assignats – that they could produce only from sixty to seventy millions per day and that the government was spending daily from eighty to ninety millions. Four thousand millions of francs were issued during one month, a little later three thousand millions, a little later four thousand millions, until there had been put forth over thirty-five thousand millions.

The purchasing power of this paper having now become almost nothing, it was decreed, on December 22, 1795, that the whole amount issued should be limited to forty thousand millions, including all that had previously been put forth and that when this had been done the copper plates should be broken. Even in spite of this, additional issues were made amounting to about ten thousand millions. But on February 18, 1796, at nine o'clock in the morning, in the presence of a great crowd, the machinery, plates, and paper for printing assignats were brought to the Place Vendome and there, on the spot where the Napoleon Column now stands, these were solemnly broken and burned.

Shortly afterward a report by Camus was made to the Assembly that the entire amount of paper money issued in less than six years by the Revolutionary Government of France had been over forty-five thousand millions of francs; that over six thousand millions had been annulled and burned; and that at the final catastrophe there were in circulation close upon forty thousand millions. It will be readily seen that it was fully time to put an end to the system, for the gold louis of twenty-five francs in specie had, in February 1796, as we have seen, become worth 7,200 francs, and, at the latest quotation of all, no less than 15,000 francs in paper money – that is, one franc in gold was nominally worth 600 francs in paper.

Such were the results of allowing dreamers, schemers, phrase-mongers, declaimers, and strong men subservient to these to control a government.[70]

How It Ended

The first new expedient of the Directory was to secure a forced loan of six hundred million francs from the wealthier classes; but this was found fruitless. Ominous it was when persons compelled to take this loan found for an assignat of one hundred francs only one franc was allowed. Next, a National Bank was proposed; but capitalists were loath to embark in banking while the howls of the mob against all who had anything especially to do with money resounded in every city. At last the Directory bethought themselves of another expedient. This was by no means new. It had been fully tried on our continent twice before that time, and once, since: first, in our colonial period; next, during our Confederation; lastly, by the 'Southern Confederacy' – and here, as elsewhere, always in vain. But experience yielded to theory – plain business sense to financial metaphysics. It was determined to issue a new paper which should be 'fully secured' and 'as good as gold.'

Pursuant to this decision it was decreed that a new paper money 'fully secured and as good as gold' be issued under the name of 'mandats'. In order that these new notes should be 'fully secured,' choice public real estate was set apart to an amount fully equal to the nominal value of the issue, and anyone offering any amount of the mandats could at once take possession of government lands, the price of the lands to be determined by two experts, one named by the government and one by the buyer, and without the formalities and delays previously established in regard to the purchase of lands and assignats.

Perhaps the most whimsical thing in the whole situation was the fact that the government, pressed as it was by demands of all sorts, continued to issue the old assignats at the same time that it was discrediting them by issuing the new mandats. And yet in order to make the mandats 'as good as gold' it was planned by forced loans and other means to reduce the quantity of assignats in circulation, so that the value of each assignat should be raised to one-thirtieth of the value of gold, then to make mandats legal tender and to substitute them for assignats at the rate of one for thirty. Never were great expectations more cruelly disappointed. Even before the mandats could be issued from the press, they fell to thirty-five per cent of their nominal value; from this they speedily fell to fifteen, and soon after to five per cent, and finally, in August 1796, six months from their first issue, to three per cent. This plan failed – just as it failed in New England in 1737; just as it failed under our own Confederation in 1781; just as it failed under the Southern Confederacy during our Civil War.[71]

To sustain this new currency the government resorted to every method that ingenuity could devise. Pamphlets suited to people of every capacity were published explaining its advantages. Never was there more skilful puffing. A pamphlet signed 'Marchant' and dedicated to 'People of Good Faith' was widely circulated, in which Marchant took pains to show the great advantage of the mandats as compared with assignats – how land could be more easily acquired with them; how their security was better than with assignats; how they could not, by any possibility, sink in values as the assignats had done. But even before the pamphlet was dry from the press the depreciation of the mandats had refuted his entire argument.[72]

The old plan of penal measures was again pressed. Monot led off by proposing penalties against those who shall speak publicly against the mandats; Talot thought the penalties ought to be made especially severe; and finally it was enacted that any persons 'who by their discourse or writing shall decry the mandats shall be condemned to a fine of not less than one thousand francs or more than ten thousand; and in case of a repetition of the offense, to four years in iron.' It was also decreed that those who refused to receive the mandats should be fined – the first time, the exact sum which they refused; the second time, ten times as much; and the third time, punished with two years in prison. But here, too, came in the action of those natural laws which are alike inexorable in all countries. This attempt proved futile in France just as it had proved futile less than twenty years before in America. No enactments could stop the downward tendency of this new paper 'fully secured,' 'as good as gold'; the laws that finally govern finance are not made in conventions or congresses.[73]

From time to time various new financial juggles were tried, some of them ingenious, most of them drastic. It was decreed that all assignats above the value of one hundred francs should cease to circulate after the beginning of June 1796. But this only served to destroy the last vestige of confidence in government notes of any kind. Another expedient was seen in the decree that paper money should be made to accord with a natural and immutable standard of value and that one franc in paper should thenceforth be worth ten pounds of wheat. This also failed. On July 16 another decree seemed to show that the authorities despaired of regulating the existing currency, and it was decreed that all paper, whether mandats or assignats, should be taken at its real value, and that bargains might be made in whatever currency people chose. The real value of the mandats speedily sank to about two per cent of their nominal value, and the only effect of this legislation seemed to be that both assignats and mandats went still lower. Then from February 4 to February 14, 1797, came decrees and orders that the engraving apparatus for the mandats should be destroyed as that for the assignats had been, that neither assignats nor mandats should longer be a legal tender, and that old debts to the state might be paid for a time with government paper at the rate of one per cent of their face value.[74] Then, less than three months later, it was decreed that the twenty-one billions of assignats still in circulation should be annulled. Finally, on September 30, 1797, as the culmination of these and various other experiments and expedients, came an order of the Directory that the national debts should be paid two-thirds in bonds which might be used in purchasing confiscated real estate, and the remaining 'Consolidated Third', as it was called, was to be placed on the 'Great Book' of the national debt to be paid thenceforth as the government should think best.

As to the bonds which the creditors of the nation were thus forced to take, they sank rapidly, as the assignats and mandats had done, even to three per cent of their value. As to the 'Consolidated Third', that was largely paid, until the coming of Bonaparte, in paper money which sank gradually to about six per cent of its face value. Since May 1797, both assignats and mandats had been virtually worth nothing.

So ended the reign of paper money in France. The twenty-five hundred millions of mandats went into the common heap of refuse with the previous forty-five thousand millions of assignats. The nation in general, rich and poor alike, was plunged into financial ruin from one end to the other.

On the prices charged for articles of ordinary use, light is thrown by extracts from a table published in 1795, reduced to American coinage.

	1790	1795
For a bushel of flour	40 cents	45 dollars
For a bushel of oats	18 cents	10 dollars
For a cartload of wood	4 dollars	500 dollars
For a bushel of coal	7 cents	2 dollars
For a pound of sugar	18 cents	$12\frac{1}{2}$ dollars
For a pound of soap	18 cents	8 dollars
For a pound of candles	18 cents	8 dollars
For one cabbage	8 cents	$5\frac{1}{2}$ dollars
For a pair of shoes	1 dollar	40 dollars
For twenty-five eggs	24 cents	5 dollars

But these prices about the middle of 1795 were moderate compared with those which were reached before the close of that year and during the year following. Perfectly authentic examples were such as the following:

A pound of bread	9 dollars
A bushel of potatoes	40 dollars
A pound of candles	40 dollars
A cartload of wood	250 dollars

So much for the poorer people. Typical of those esteemed wealthy may be mentioned a manufacturer of hardware who, having retired from business in 1790 with 321,000 livres, found his property in 1796 worth 14,000 francs.[75]

From this general distress arising from the development and collapse of 'fiat' money in France, there was, indeed, one exception. In Paris and a few of the other great cities, men like Tallien, of the heartless, debauched, luxurious, speculator, contractor, and stock-gambler class, had risen above the ruins of the multitudes of smaller fortunes. Tallien, one of the worst demagogue 'reformers', and a certain number of men like him, had been skilful enough to become millionaires, while their dupes, who had clamoured for issues of paper money, had become paupers.

The luxury and extravagance of the currency gamblers and their families form one of the most significant features in any picture of the social condition of that period.[76]

A few years before this the leading women in French society showed a nobility of character and a simplicity in dress worthy of

Roman matrons. Of these were Madame Roland and Madame Desmoulins; but now all was changed. At the head of society stood Madame Tallien and others like her, wild in extravagance, daily seeking new refinements in luxury, and demanding of their husbands and lovers vast sums to array them and to feed their whims. If such sums could not be obtained honestly, they must be had dishonestly. The more closely one examines that period, the more clearly he sees that the pictures given by Thibaudeau and Challamel and De Goncourt are not at all exaggerated.[77]

The contrast between these gay creatures of the Directory period and the people at large was striking. Indeed, much as the vast majority of the wealthy classes suffered from impoverishment, the labouring classes, salaried employees of all sorts, and people of fixed income and of small means, especially in the cities, underwent yet greater distress. These were found, as a rule, to subsist mainly on daily government rations of bread at the rate of one pound per person. This was frequently unfit for food and was distributed to long lines of people, men, women, and children, who were at times obliged to wait their turn even from dawn to dusk. The very rich could, by various means, especially by bribery, obtain better bread, but only at enormous cost. In May 1796, the market price of good bread was, in paper, 80 francs (16 dollars) per pound and a little later provisions could not be bought for paper money at any price.[78]

And here it may be worth mentioning that there was another financial trouble especially vexatious. While, as we have seen, such enormous sums, rising from twenty to forty thousand millions of francs in paper, were put in circulation by the successive governments of the Revolution, enormous sums had been set afloat in counterfeits by criminals and by the enemies of France. These came not only from various parts of the French Republic but from nearly all the surrounding nations, the main source being London. Thence it was that Count Joseph de Puisaye sent off cargoes of false paper, excellently engraved and printed, through ports in Brittany and other disaffected parts of France. One seizure by General Hoche was declared by him to exceed in nominal value ten thousand millions of francs. With the exception of a few of these issues, detection was exceedingly difficult, even for experts; for the vast majority of the people it was impossible.

Nor was this all. At various times the insurgent royalists in La Vendee and elsewhere put *their* presses also in operation, issuing notes bearing the Bourbon arms – the *fleur-de-lis*, the portrait of the Dauphin (as Louis XVII) with the magic legend *'De Par le Roi,'* and large bodies of the population in the insurgent districts were *forced* to take these. Even as late as 1799 these notes continued to appear.[79]

The financial agony was prolonged somewhat by attempts to secure funds by still another 'forced loan,' and other discredited measures; but when all was over with paper money, specie began to reappear – first in sufficient sums to do the small amount of business which remained after the collapse. Then as the business demand increased, the amount of specie flowed in from the world at large to meet it, and the nation gradually recovered from that long paper money debauch.

Thibaudeau, a very thoughtful observer, tells us in his Memoirs that great fears were felt as to a want of circulating medium between the time when paper should go out and coin should come in; but that no such want was severely felt – that coin came in gradually as it was wanted.[80]

Nothing could better exemplify the saying of one of the most shrewd of modern statesmen that 'there will always be money'.[81]

But though there soon came a degree of prosperity – as compared with the distress during the paper money orgy —— convalescence was slow. The acute suffering from the wreck and ruin brought by assignats, mandats, and other paper currency in process of repudiation lasted nearly ten years, but the period of recovery lasted longer than the generation which followed. It required fully forty years to bring capital, industry, commerce, and credit up to their condition when the Revolution began, and demanded a 'man on horseback', who established monarchy on the ruins of the Republic and threw away millions of lives for the Empire, to be added to the millions which had been sacrificed by the Revolution.[82]

Such, briefly sketched in its leading features, is the history of the most skilful, vigorous, and persistent attempt ever made to substitute for natural laws in finance the ability of legislative bodies, and, for a standard of value recognized throughout the world, a national standard devised by theorists and manipulated by schemers. Every other attempt of the same kind in human history, under whatever circumstances, has reached similar results in kind if not in degree; all of them show the existence of financial laws as real in their operation as those which hold the planets in their courses.[83]

I have now presented this history in its *chronological* order – the order of events. Let me, in conclusion, sum it up, briefly, in its *logical order* – the order of cause and effect.

And, first, in the *economic* department. From the early reluctant and careful issues of paper we saw, as an immediate result, improvement and activity in business. Then arose the clamour for more paper money. At first, new issues were made with great difficulty; but, the dike once broken, the current of irredeemable currency poured through; and, the breach thus enlarging, this currency was soon swollen beyond control. It was urged on by speculators for a rise in values; by demagogues who persuaded the mob that a nation, by its simple fiat, could stamp real value to any amount upon valueless objects. As a natural consequence, a great debtor class grew rapidly, and this class gave its influence to depreciate more and more the currency in which its debts were to be paid.[84]

The government now began, and continued by spasms to grind out still more paper; commerce was at first stimulated by the difference in exchange; but this cause soon ceased to operate, and commerce, having been stimulated unhealthfully, wasted away.

Manufactures at first received a great impulse; but, ere long, this overproduction and overstimulus proved as fatal to them as to commerce. From time to time there was a revival of hope caused by an apparent revival of business; but this revival of business was at last seen to be caused more and more by the desire of far-seeing and cunning men of affairs to exchange paper money for objects of permanent value. As to the people at large, the classes living on fixed incomes and small salaries felt the pressure first, as soon as the purchasing power of their fixed incomes was reduced. Soon the great class living on wages felt it even more sadly.

Prices of the necessities of life increased. Merchants were obliged to increase them, not only to cover depreciation of their merchandise, but also to cover their risk of loss from fluctuation; and, while the prices of products thus rose, wages, which had at first gone up, under the general stimulus, lagged behind. Under the universal doubt and discouragement, commerce and manufactures were checked or destroyed. As a consequence, the demand for labour was diminished; labouring men were thrown out of employment; and, under the operation of the simplest law of supply and demand, the price of labour – the daily wages of the labouring class – went down until, at a time when prices of food, clothing, and various articles of consumption were enormous, wages were nearly as low as at the time preceding the first issue of irredeemable currency.

The mercantile classes at first thought themselves exempt from the general misfortune. They were delighted at the apparent advance in the value of the goods upon their shelves. But they soon found that, as they increased prices to cover the inflation of currency and the risk from fluctuation and uncertainty, purchases became less in amount and payments less secure; a feeling of insecurity spread throughout the country; enterprise was deadened and stagnation followed.

New issues of paper were then clamoured for as more drams are demanded by a drunkard. New issues only increased the evil; capitalists were all the more reluctant to embark their money on such a sea of doubt. Workmen of all sorts were more and more thrown out of employment. Issue after issue of currency came; but no relief resulted save a momentary stimulus which aggravated the disease. The most ingenious evasions of natural laws in finance which the most subtle theorists could contrive were tried – all in vain; the most brilliant substitutes for those laws were tried; 'self-regulating' schemes, 'interconverting' schemes – all equally vain.[85] All thoughtful men had lost confidence. All men were *waiting*; stagnation became worse and worse. At last came the collapse and then a return, by a fearful shock, to a state of things which presented something like certainty of remuneration to capital and labour. Then, and not till then, came the beginning of a new era of prosperity.

Just as dependent on the law of cause and effect was the *moral* development. Out of the inflation of prices grew a speculating class; and, in the complete uncertainty as to the future, all business became a game of chance, and all businessmen, gamblers. In city centres came a quick growth of stockjobbers and speculators; and these set a debasing fashion in business which spread to the remotest parts of the country. Instead of satisfaction with legitimate profits, came a passion for inordinate gains. Then, too, as values became more and more uncertain, there was no longer any motive for care or economy, but every motive for immediate expenditure and present enjoyment. So came upon the nation the *obliteration of thrift*. In this mania for yielding to present enjoyment rather than providing for future comfort were the seeds of new growths of wretchedness: luxury, senseless and extravagant, set in. This, too, spread as a fashion. To feed it, there came cheatery in the nation at large and corruption among officials and persons holding trusts. While men set such fashions in private and official business, women set fashions of extravagance in dress and living that added to the incentives to corruption. Faith in moral considerations, or even in good impulses, yielded to general distrust. National honour was thought a fiction cherished only by hypocrites. Patriotism was eaten out by cynicism.

Thus was the history of France logically developed in obedience to natural laws; such has, to a greater or less degree, always been the result of irredeemable paper, created according to the whim or interest of legislative assemblies rather than based upon standards of value permanent in their nature and agreed upon throughout the entire world. Such, we may fairly expect, will always be the result of them until the fiat of the Almighty shall evolve laws in the universe radically different from those which at present obtain.[86]

And, finally, as to the general development of the theory and practice which all this history records: my subject has been Fiat Money Inflation in France: how it came; what it brought; and how it ended.

It came by seeking a remedy for a comparatively small evil in an evil infinitely more dangerous. To cure a disease temporary in its character, a corrosive poison was administered, which ate out the vitals of French prosperity.

It progressed according to a law in social physics which we may call the 'law of accelerating issue and depreciation.' It was comparatively easy to refrain from the first issue; it was exceedingly difficult to refrain from the second; to refrain from the third and those following was practically impossible.

It brought, as we have seen, commerce and manufactures, the mercantile interest, the agricultural interest, to ruin. It brought on these the same destruction which would come to a Hollander opening the dikes of the sea to irrigate his garden in a dry summer.

It ended in the complete financial, moral, and political prostration of France – a prostration from which only a Napoleon could raise it.

But this history would be incomplete without a brief sequel, showing how that great genius profited by all his experience. When

Bonaparte took the consulship, the condition of fiscal affairs was appalling. The government was bankrupt; an immense debt was unpaid. The further collection of taxes seemed impossible; the assessments were in hopeless confusion. War was going on in the East, on the Rhine, and in Italy, and civil war, in La Vendée. All the armies had long been unpaid, and the largest loan that could for the moment be effected was for a sum hardly meeting the expenses of the government for a single day. At the first cabinet council Bonaparte was asked what he intended to do. He replied, 'I will pay cash or pay nothing.' From this time he conducted all his operations on this basis. He arranged the assessments, funded the debt, and made payments in cash; and from this time – during all the campaigns of Marengo, Austerlitz, Jena, Eylau, Friedland, down to the peace of Tilsit in 1807 – there was but one suspension of specie payment, and this only for a few days.

When the first great European coalition was formed against the Empire, Napoleon was hard pressed financially, and it was proposed to resort to paper money; but he wrote to his minister, 'While I live, I will never resort to irredeemable paper.' He never did, and France, under this determination, commanded all the gold she needed. When Waterloo came, with the invasion of the Allies, with war on her own soil, with a change of dynasty, and with heavy expenses for war and indemnities, France, on a specie basis, experienced no severe financial distress.

If we glance at the financial history of France, during the Franco-Prussian War, and the communist struggle in which a far more serious pressure was brought upon French finances than our own recent Civil War put upon American finance, and yet with no national stagnation or distress but with a steady progress in prosperity, we shall see still more clearly the advantage of meeting a financial crisis in an honest and straightforward way, and by methods sanctioned by the world's most costly experience, rather than by yielding to dreamers, theorists, phrase-mongers, declaimers, schemers, speculators, or to that sort of 'Reform' which is 'the last refuge of a scoundrel.'[87]

There is a lesson in all this which it behoves every thinking man to ponder.

CHRONOLOGICAL TABLE

		Assignats in circulation (millions of livres or francs)
	1789	
May 5	An attempt to cure the bankrupt state of the public treasury caused Louis XVI to call a meeting of the States-General, which later amalgamated into the single-chamber National Assembly	
July 14	Fall of the Bastille, after several days of rioting in Paris	
October 5	Declaration of the Rights of Man adopted by Assembly	
November 2	Confiscation of church property	
	1790	
April	First issue of paper assignats, 400 million livres	400
September 29	Second issue, 800 million	1,200
	1791	
June 19	Third issue, 600 million	1,800
September	New Constitution; National Assembly dissolved and replaced by Legislative Assembly	
December 17	Fourth issue, 300 million	2,100
	1792	
April 30	Fifth issue, 300 million	2,400
	France at war with Russia and Austria	
June-August	Riots in Paris; King dethroned and royal family imprisoned; Revolutionary Commune takes power; more assignats	2,700
September	Election of National Convention replacing Legislative Assembly; Monarchy abolished; government by	

		Assignats in circulation (millions of livres or francs)
	committees; political corruption	
December 14	Total assignats issued to date 3,400 million; 600 million destroyed	2,800
	1793	
January 21	Louis XVI beheaded	
January 31	More assignats	3,000
February-March	Formation of Committee of Public Safety; rioting in Paris over high prices; Revolutionary Tribunal established; Reign of Terror begins	
May 3	Price control on grains	
June 22	Forced Loan decreed – a progressive income tax	
August 1	Trading in specie prohibited	
September 29	Law of the Maximum – price control extended to all food	
October 16	Marie Antoinette beheaded – Over 3,000 million new assignats issued during the year, of which 1,200 million entered circulation	4,200
	1794	
June 4	Robespierre elected president of National Convention; thousands executed by decree of Revolutionary Tribunal	
July 27	Robespierre beheaded; end of Reign of Terror	
December	Law of Maximum repealed	
	Assignats in circulation at end of year	7,000
	1795	
May 31	Assignats in circulation	14,000
	More rioting; business and trade	

		Assignats in circulation (millions of livres or francs)
	disrupted; shortages persist; uncertain government	
July 31	Assignats in circulation	14,000
September 23	New Constitution adopted and new government formed – the Directory	35,000
	1796	
February 18	Machinery, plates, and paper for printing assignats destroyed	40,000
	First issue of new paper notes – mandats – to displace assignats at 30:1	
August	Mandats worth only 3 per cent of face value; about 2,500 million mandats issued altogether	
	1797	
February	Legal tender qualities withdrawn from both assignats and mandats, which became worthless after May	
	1798	
	Arbitrary government by the Directory; business disrupted; people discontented; Napoleon gaining military victories abroad	
	1799	
November 10	Napoleon comes into power – 'to save the Republic'	

Footnotes

1. For proof that the financial situation of France at that time was by no means hopeless, see Storch, *Economie Politique*, vol. iv., p. 159.
2. See *Moniteur*, sitting of April 10, 1790.

3. *Ibid.*, sitting of April 15, 1790.
4. For details of this struggle, see Buchez and Roux, *Histoire parlementaire de la Révolution française*, vol. iii, pp. 364, 365, 404. For the wild utterances of Marat throughout this whole history, see the full set of his *L'ami du peuple* in the President White Collection of the Cornell University Library. For Bergasse's pamphlet and a mass of similar publications, see the same collection. For the effect produced by them, see Challamel, *Les Français sous la Révolution*; also De Goncourt, *La Société française pendant la Révolution*, etc. For the Report referred to, see Levasseur, *Histoire des classes ouvrierès et de l'industrie en France de 1789 à 1870*, Paris, 1903, vol. i, chap. 6. Levasseur (vol. 1, p. 120), a very strong conservative in such estimates, sets the total value of church property at two thousand millions; other authorities put it as high as twice that sum. See especially Taine, vol. ii, chap. I, who gives the valuation as 'about four milliards'. Von Sybel, *Geschichte der Revolutionzeit*, gives it as two milliards and Briand, *La séparation*, etc., agrees with him. See also De Nervo, *Finances françaises*, vol. ii, pp. 236-240; also Alison, *History of Europe*, vol. i.
5. For striking pictures of this feeling among the younger generation of Frenchmen, see Challamel, *Sur la Révolution*, p. 305. For general history of John Law's paper money, see Henri Martin, *Histoire de France*; also Blanqui, *Histoire de l'économie politique*, vol. ii, pp. 65-87; also Senior on *Paper Money*, sec. iii, Pt. 1; also Thiers, *Histoire de Law*; also Levasseur, *op. cit.*, vol. i, chap. VI. Several specimens of John Law's paper currency are to be found in the White Collection in the Cornell University Library – some numbered with enormous figures.
6. See Buchez and Roux, *Histoire parlementaire*, vol. v, p. 321, *et seq.* For an argument to prove that the assignats were, after all, not so well secured as John Law's money, see Storch, *Economie Politique*, vol. iv, p. 160.
7. For specimens of this first issue and of nearly every other issue during the French Revolution, see the extensive collection of originals in the Cornell University Library. For a virtually complete collection of photographic copies, see Dewarmin, *Cent ans de numismatique française*, vol. i, passim.
8. See *Addresse de l'Assemblée nationale sur les emissions d'assignats monnaies*, p. 5.
9. *Ibid.*, p. 10.
10. For Sarot, see *Lettre de M. Sarot*, Paris, April 19, 1790. As to the sermon referred to, see Levasseur, as above, vol. i, p. 136.
11. Von Sybel, *History of the French Revolution*, vol. i, p. 252; also Levasseur, as above, pp. 137 and following.
12. For Mirabeau's real opinion on irredeemable paper, see his letter to Cerutti, in a leading article of the *Moniteur*; also *Mémoires de Mirabeau*, vol. vii, pp. 23, 24, and elsewhere. For his pungent remarks above quoted, see Levasseur, *op. cit.*, vol. i, p. 118.
13. See *Moniteur*, August 27, 1790.
14. *Moniteur*, August 28, 1790; also Levasseur, as above, pp. 139, *et seq.*
15. *Par une seule opération, grande, simple, magnifique.* See *Moniteur*. The whole sounds curiously like the proposals of the Greenbackers, regarding the American debt, some years since.
16. *Moniteur*, August 29, 1790.
17. See Lacretelle, *Histoire de France pendant le XVIII siécle*, vol. viii, pp. 84-87; also Thiers and Mignet.

18. See Hatin, *Histoire de la Presse en France*, vol. v and vi.
19. See *Moniteur*, Sept. 5, 6, and 20, 1790.
20. See Levasseur, vol. i, p. 142.
21. See speech in *Moniteur*; also in Appendix to Thiers' *History of the French Revolution.*
22. See Levasseur, *Classes ouvrières*, etc., vol. i., p. 149.
23. See Levasseur, pp. 151 *et seq*. Various examples of these 'confidence bills' are to be seen in the Cornell University Library.
24. See Levasseur, vol. i, pp. 155-156.
25. See Von Sybel, *History of the Revolution*, vol. i, p. 265; also Levasseur, as above, vol. i, pp. 152-160.
26. For Turgot's argument against 'fiat money' theory, see A.D. White, *Seven Great Statesmen in the Warfare of Humanity with Unreason*, article on Turgot, pp. 169, *et seq.*
27. See De Goncourt, *Société française,* for other explanations; *Les Révolutions de Paris*, vol. ii, p. 216; Challamel, *Les Français sous la Révolution*; Senior, *On Some Effects of Paper Money*, p. 82; Buchez and Roux, *Histoire parlementaire*, etc., vol. x, p. 216; Aulard, *Paris pendant la réaction thermidorienne*, passim, and especially *Rapport du bureau de surveillance*, vol. ii, pp. 562, *et seq.* (Dec. 4-24, 1795).
28. For statements and illustration of the general action of this law, see Sumner, *History of American Currency,* pp. 157, 158; also Jevons, on *Money*, p. 80.
29. See De Goncourt, *Société française*, p. 214.
30. See Von Sybel, *History of the French Revolution*, vol. i, pp. 281, 283.
31. For proofs that issues of irredeemable paper at first stimulated manufactures and commerce in Austria and afterward ruined them, see Storch's *Economie Politique*, vol. iv, p. 223, note; and for the same effect produced by the same causes in Russia, see *ibid.*, end of vol. iv. For the same effects in America, see Sumner's *History of American Currency*. For general statement of effect of inconvertible issues on foreign exchanges, see McLeod on *Banking*, p. 186.
32. See Louis Blanc, *Histoire de la Révolution française*, tome xii, p. 113.
33. See *Extrait du registre des délibérations de la section de la bibliothèque*, May 3, 1791, pp. 4, 5.
34. Von Sybel, vol. i, p. 273.
35. For general account, see Thiers' *Révolution*, chap. xiv; also Lacretelle, vol. viii, p. 109; also *Memoirs of Mallet du Pan*. For a good account of the intrigues between the court and Mirabeau and of the prices paid him, see Reeve, *Democracy and Monarchy in France*, vol. i, pp. 213-220. For a very striking caricature published after the iron chest in the Tuileries was opened and the evidences of bribery of Mirabeau fully revealed, see Challamel, *Musée*, etc., vol. i, p. 341. Mirabeau is represented as a skeleton sitting on a pile of letters, holding the French crown in one hand and a purse of gold in the other.
36. Thiers, chap. ix.
37. For this and other evidences of steady decline in the purchasing power of the assignats, see Caron, *Tableaux de Dépréciation du papier-monnaie*, Paris, 1909, p. 386.
38. See especially *Discours de Fabre d'Eglantine*, in *Moniteur* for August 11, 1793; also debate in *Moniteur* of September 15, 1793; also Prudhomme's *Révolutions de Paris*. For arguments of much the same tenor, see vast

number of pamphlets, newspaper articles, and speeches during the 'Greenback Craze' – and the craze for unlimited coinage of silver – in the United States.

39. See Caron, *Tableaux de Dépréciation*, as above, p. 386.
40. Von Sybel, vol. i, pp. 509, 510, 515; also Villeneuve Bargemont, *Histoire de l'economie politique*, vol. ii, p. 213.
41. As to the purchasing power of money at that time, see Arthur Young, *Travels in France during the Years 1787, 1788,* and *1789*. For notices of the small currency with examples of satirical verses written regarding it, see Challamel, *Les Français sous la Révolution*, pp. 307, 308. See also Mercier, *Le Nouveau Paris*, edition of 1800, chapter ccv, entitled 'Parchemin Monnaie.' A series of these petty notes will be found in the White Collection of the Cornell University Library. They are very dirty and much worn, but being printed on parchment, remain perfectly legible. For issue of quarter-sou pieces, see Levasseur, p. 180.
42. See Levasseur, vol. i, p. 176.
43. For Chaumette's brilliant display of fictitious reasons for the decline, see Thiers, Shobel's translation, published by Bentley, vol. iii, p. 248.
44. For these fluctuations, see Caron, as above, p. 387.
45. One of the Forced Loan certificates will be found in the White Collection in the Library of Cornell University.
46. For details of these transactions, see Levasseur, as above, vol. i, chap. 6, pp. 181, *et seq*. Original specimens of these notes, bearing the portrait of Louis XVI will be found in the Cornell University Library (White Collection) and for the whole series perfectly photographed in the same collection, Dewarmin, *Cent ans de numismatique française*, vol. i, pp. 143-165.
47. For statements showing the distress and disorder that forced the Convention to establish the 'Maximum', see Levasseur, vol. i, pp. 188-193.
48. See Levasseur, as above, vol. i, pp. 195-225.
49. See specimens of these tickets in the White Collection in the Cornell Library.
50. For these condemnations to the guillotine, see the officially published trials and also the lists of the condemned, in the White Collection, also the lists given daily in the *Moniteur*. For the spy system, see Levasseur, vol. i, p. 194.
51. See Levasseur, as above, vol. i, p. 186. For an argument to show that the Convention was led into this Draconian legislation, not by necessity, but by its despotic tendencies. see Von Sybel's *History of the French Revolution*, vol. iii, pp. 11, 12. For general statements of theories underlying the Maximum, see Thiers; for a very interesting picture, by an eye-witness, of the absurdities and miseries it caused, see Mercier, *Le Nouveau Paris*, edition of 1800, chapter XLIV.
52. For a summary of the report of the Committee, with list of articles embraced under it, and for various interesting details, see Villeneuve Bargemont, *Histoire de l'economie politique*, vol. ii, pp. 213-239; also Levasseur, as above. For curious examples of severe penalties for very slight infringements on the law on the subject, see Louis Blanc, *Histoire de la Révolution française*, tome x, p. 144. For Louis XIV's claim, see *Memoirs of Louis XIV for the Instruction of the Dauphin*.

    For a simple exposition of the way in which the exercise of this power became simply confiscation of all private property in France, see Mallet du Pan's *Memoirs*, London, 1852, vol. ii, p. 14.
53. See Du Pont's arguments, as given by Levasseur.

54. Louis Blanc calls attention to this very fact in showing the superiority of the French assignats to the old American Continental currency. See his *Histoire de la Révolution française*, tome xii, p. 98.
55. See Sumner, as above, p. 220.
56. See Levasseur, as above, vol. i, p. 178.
57. See Cambon's *Report*, Aug. 15, 1793, pp. 49-60; also, *Decree of Aug. 24, 1793*, sec. 31, chapters XCVI-CIII. Also, *Tableaux de la Dépréciation de papier monnaie dans le department de la Seine.*
58. For the example of Metz and other authorities, see Levasseur, as above, vol. i, p. 180.
59. See Von Sybel, vol. iii, p. 173.
60. See Thiers; also, for curious details of measures taken to compel farmers and merchants, see Senior, Lectures on *Results of Paper Money*, pp. 86, 87.
61. See Von Sybel, vol. iv, p. 231.
62. See Von Sybel, vol. iv, p. 330; also tables of depreciation in *Moniteur*; also official reports in the White Collection; also Caron's *Tableaux*, etc.
63. For a lifelike sketch of the way in which these exchanges of assignats for valuable property went on at periods of the rapid depreciation of paper, see Challamel, *Les Français sous la Révolution*, p. 309; also see *Economie Politique*.
64. For a very complete table of the depreciation from day to day, see *Supplement to the Moniteur* of October 2, 1797; also Caron, as above. For the market prices of the *louis d'or* at the first of every month, as the collapse approached, see Montgaillard. See also 'Official Lists' in the White Collection. For a table showing the steady rise of the franc in gold during a single week, from 251 to 280 francs, see Dewarmin, as above, vol. i, p. 136.
65. See *Mémoires de Tribaudeau*, vol. ii, p. 26, also Mercier, *Le Nouveau Paris*, vol. ii, p. 90; for curious example of the scales of depreciation, see the White Collection. See also extended table of comparative values in 1790 and 1795. See Levasseur, as above, vol. i, pp. 223-224.
66. For a striking similar case in our own country, see Sumner, *History of American Currency*, p. 47.
67. See Villeneuve Bargemont, *Histoire de l'économie politique*, vol. ii, p. 229.
68. See Von Sybel, vol. iv, pp. 337, 338. See also for confirmation Challamel, *Histoire Musée*, vol. ii, p. 179. For a thoughtful statement of the reasons why such paper was not invested in lands by men of moderate means, and workingmen, see Mill, *Political Economy*, vol. ii, pp. 81, 82.
69. See Von Sybel, vol. iv, p. 222.
70. See especially Levasseur, *Histoire des classes ouvrières*, etc., vol. i, pp. 219, 230, and elsewhere; also De Nervo, *Finance française*, p. 280; also Stourm, as already cited. The exact amount of assignats in circulation at the final suppression is given by Derwarmin, (vol. i, p. 189), as 39,999,945,428 livres or francs.
71. For details of the mandat system very thoroughly given, see Thiers' *History of the French Revolution*, Bentley's edition, vol. iv, pp. 410-412. For the issue of assignats and mandats at the same time, see Derwarmin, vol. i, p. 136; also Levasseur, vol. i, pp. 230-257. For an account of 'new tenor bills' in America and their failure in 1737, see Sumner, pp. 27-31; for their failure in 1781, see Morse, *Life of Alexander Hamilton*, vol. i, pp. 86, 87. For similar failure in Austria, see Sumner, p. 314.
72. See Marchant, *Lettre aux gens de bonne foi.*

73. See Sumner, p. 44; also De Nervo, *Finances françaises*, p. 282.
74. See De Nervo, *Finance françaises*, p. 282; also Levasseur, vol. i, p. 236, *et seq*.
75. See Table from *Gazette de France* and extracts from other sources in Levasseur, vol. i, pp. 223-224.
76. Among the many striking accounts of the debasing effects of 'inflation' upon France under the Directory, perhaps the best is that of Lacretelle, vol. xiii, pp. 32-36. For similar effect, produced by the same cause in our own country in 1819, see statement from Niles's *Register*, in Sumner, p. 80. For the jumble of families reduced to beggary with families lifted into sudden wealth and for the mass of folly and misery thus mingled, see Levasseur, vol. i, p. 237.
77. For Madame Tallien and luxury of the stock-gambler classes, see Challamel, *Les Français sous la Révolution*, pp. 30, 33; also De Goncourt, *Les Français sous le Directoire*. Regarding the outburst of vice in Paris and the demoralization of the police, see Levasseur, as above.
78. See Levasseur, vol. i, p. 237, *et seq*.
79. For specimens of counterfeit assignats, see the White Collection in the Cornell University Library, but for the great series of various issues of them in facsimile, also for detective warnings and attempted descriptions of many varieties of them, and for the history of their issue, see especially Dewarmin, vol. i, pp. 152-161. For photographic copies of Royalist assignats, etc., see also Dewarmin, *ibid*., pp. 192-197, etc. For a photograph of probably the last of the Royalist notes ever issued, bearing the words *Pro Deo, pro Rege, pro Patria* and *Armée Catholique et Royale* with the date 1799, and for the sum of 100 livres, see Dewarmin, vol. i, p. 204.
80. For similar expectation of a 'shock,' which did not occur, at the resumption of specie payments in Massachusetts, see Sumner, *History of American Currency*, p. 34.
81. See Thiers.
82. See Levasseur, vol. i, p. 246.
83. For examples of similar effects in Russia, Austria, and Denmark, see Storch, *Economie Politique*, vol. iv; for similar effects in the United States, see Gouge, *Paper Money and Banking in the United States*; also Sumner, *History of American Currency*. For working out of the same principles in England, depicted in a masterly way, see Macaulay, *History of England*, chap. xxi; and for curious exhibition of the same causes producing same results in ancient Greece, see a curious quotation by Macaulay in same chapter.
84. For parallel cases in the early history of our own country, see Sumner, p. 21, and elsewhere.
85. For a review of some of these attempts with eloquent statement of their evil results, see *Mémoires de Durand de Maillane*, pp. 166-169.
86. For similar effect of inflated currency in enervating and undermining trade, husbandry, manufactures, and morals in our own country, see Daniel Webster, cited in Sumner, pp. 45-50. For similar effects in other countries, see Senior, Storch, Macaulay, and others already cited.
87. For facts regarding French finance under Napoleon, I am indebted to Hon. David A. Wells. For more recent triumphs of financial common sense in France, see Bonnet's articles, translated by the late George Walker, Esq. For general subject, see Levasseur.

THE WITCHES' SABBATH

Thomas Mann
translated by Ralph Manheim

GERMANY 1923

The German Inflation had its roots in the First World War which was ruinously costly, not only in terms of human lives, but of labour and raw materials as well. Day after day, year in, year out, fortunes were spent. At the same time numerous commodities that Germany had imported before the War vanished from the market. More currency was in circulation because more men – and women – than usual were working. The Germans became poorer in tangible goods and richer in banknotes. ...

What was the popular reaction to this state of affairs? Since no one knew what the future would bring, since most people had no one to save for because their sons, husbands, and brothers were at the Front and might never return, and since the rising cost of living made saving next to impossible in any case, they bought whatever they could lay hands on regardless of the price. A pound of rancid butter brought 20 marks on the black market, which began to play a critical role in almost every German household. It came to be regarded as normal and even honourable to break the law by exceeding one's rations and spending unconscionable sums on illegal purchases.

In my own home we were relatively law-abiding. I say relatively, because it was becoming almost impossible to live on what the law allowed, for one thing because unscrupulous and insatiable black marketeers diverted so many goods from the already understocked legal market.

The black marketeers – sinister, repellent figures – would come in the evening and talk in whispers to my wife in the vestibule. 'For heaven's sake, Herr Hirsch', my wife would say, 'forty pfennings for an egg! Why, last week it was only thirty. What are we coming to?'

The black marketeer, a shady young man of nineteen or twenty, too sickly no doubt to serve at the front, but vigorous enough to intimidate my wife who in a way was dependent on him, laughed. 'Don't be a fool', he said, 'I could ask 50 pfennings if I wanted, or 60 or 70. You need the stuff. You have four children. They have to eat, don't they?'

And so my wife bought four of his expensive eggs. She should have taken eight, for at his next visit, a week later, Herr Hirsch had raised his prices considerably. As a matter of fact he had stopped calling himself Hirsch; now he was Herr Rabenstein – actually von Rabenstein, if I remember right.

Hirsch von Rabenstein and company on the one hand, and their customers, the German people, on the other helped to bring German inflation into the world, though it also had other midwives who are well known to us. During the War, to be sure, we didn't call it 'inflation'. We merely complained of the 'rising prices' on the legal and illegal markets. We didn't know yet that the disproportion between demand and supply, between the amount of currency in circulation and the amount of commodities available would increase according to a malignant inherent law.

The Blockade ended with the War. Rationing and other wartime restrictions were lifted. But Germany had lost its immense foreign holdings, its industry was at a standstill, and the demands of the victor powers made deep inroads on the country's remaining wealth; Germany had lost the confidence of the world and its self-confidence as well. These conditions gave rise to what was then known as the 'rush for material goods.'

The buying spree that had begun during the War surpassed all bounds afterwards. For fear of currency devaluation, people bought everything in sight – it never occurred to them that in so doing they were helping to devalue the already devalued currency still further. All Germany became one enormous black market. ...

Once the mechanism of Inflation has been set in motion it is hard to stop. Any attempt on the part of individuals to oppose it is like trying to stop Niagara Falls with an umbrella. The war against Inflation, if it is to succeed, must be a preventive war. On the other hand, economic factors alone would not have sufficed to reduce the

German mark, not to a tenth or a hundredth but to a billionth of its former value; political and psychological factors were also at work.

The German penchant for immoderation, for catastrophic irrationality, which since then has brought such unspeakable suffering on the world, was evident even then. Equally evident was the willingness of the German people to put up with whatever their ruling class saw fit. For at least a section of this ruling class, the big industrialists, the inflation was profitable; they were in no hurry to stop it. During those years the Krupps, Stinneses, Thyssens, etc., got rid of their indebtedness, which ran into real millions, by paying their creditors in inflation millions, and thanks to these same inflation millions they acquired real millions-worth of property.

Though Germany was very poor at that time, it possessed great wealth in mineral resources and industrial plant. During the Inflation a radical change occurred; this wealth became concentrated in fewer and fewer hands. The small and medium property-owners lost their holdings, and the biggest snapped them up. They acquired property and paid with paper. Years later one could hear it said that such and such a factory or mine was unproductive and would not be profitable if it had not been acquired for next-to-nothing during the Inflation. ...

Never have those who wanted to make money without working found such favourable conditions as in Germany from 1922 to 1924. All that was needed was a certain degree of ingenuity and unscrupulousness. Honest work, however skilled, brought nothing. Consequently, even ordinarily honest people were infected with the fever of speculation. Peasants filled their houses with sewing machines, pianos, and Persian rugs, and refused to part with their eggs and milk except in exchange for articles of permanent value. Medical students became stock-jobbers. Teachers discussed such topics with their classes as how to convert a little money into a lot of money. The answer: by buying foreign currency, holding it for a while and then reselling it. In that way a million could be turned into five millions and ultimately into a billion.

But hadn't prices risen correspondingly in the meantime? For the most part, yes, but not necessarily; not if you took your money as fast as your legs would carry you to some innocent grocer or wine dealer or artist. If you were lucky, he had the mark quotation for 9 a.m., but not for 12 noon; the difference – to his disadvantage –

could be enormous. On the other hand, if he was a little less innocent he might ring up his bank, sigh, wipe the perspiration from his forehead, and rectify his prices. Yes, the purchaser could also be the loser. For instance, you might drop in at the tobacconist's for a cigar. Alarmed at the price, you'd rush to a competitor, find that his price was still higher, and race back to the first shop, which may have doubled or tripled its price in the meantime. There was no help for it, you had to dig into your pocketbook and take out a huge bundle of millions, or even billions, depending on the date. …

On Friday evenings you could see workers coming out of the factories with baskets, sacks, and suitcases full of money. It didn't do them much good, for the frightened and greedy shopkeepers often raised their prices faster than the value of the currency fell. It became necessary to pay wages daily, and in the end the firm of Krupp among others began to print its own bank-notes. The cities, even the smallest of them, also took to printing money; it was up to some high official to decide how much. It goes without saying that for the time being forgery ceased to exist as a trade.

Large profits could be made by borrowing money. Anyone who had borrowed money in 1920 and bought something substantial – a house, a farm, or a factory – was well off in 1923. The lender was not so fortunate. Shrewd and far-sighted individuals leapt at the opportunity to victimize old-fashioned people who failed to understand the spirit of the times. Of these there were only too many. How could a man who in his youth had reckoned in thalers, gulden, kurant marks, and later on in Bismarck's gilt-edged reichsmarks, be expected to think in terms of billions and trillions in his old age?

I can still remember the look of pride on our old governess's face when she told us one day that she was planning to retire soon and live on her savings. At the time the few thousand marks she had in the bank were worth less than a penny. People who had once been wealthy and were still living in their dilapidated old mansions sold their art treasures and furniture to sharpers. A Rembrandt might bring them enough to live on for a few weeks. In the end they were turned out into the streets with their pockets full of worthless multi-coloured paper.

In those days you had to keep abreast of the times to survive. Sometimes you were cheated without malice aforethought. During the War I had invested ten thousand marks in a friend's country house, where I was a frequent guest. In a sense I was part-owner of the house. For practical purposes, my loan of ten thousand marks was guaranteed by a lien on the house. In the spring of 1923 my friend informed me that circumstances had obliged him to sell his house, so he was returning my money. As a matter of fact, he added with a smile, it was the same ten thousand, the same banknotes, I had given him in 1917; they had been lying untouched in his safe all the while. There I stood, incredulous, baffled and embarrassed, holding the clean, almost new, handsomely engraved museum pieces.

Those who joined in the 'rush for material goods' didn't necessarily fare any better. I can think of no one in my circle of acquaintances who succeeded in weathering the inflation with all his possessions intact. And most of the new fortunes amassed by adventurers vanished as quickly as they had come into being. That is the main reason why I have always regarded the German Inflation as a kind of mirage, a witches' sabbath, that vanished, leaving nothing behind it but headaches and regrets. In the summer of 1923 the Inflation, like the legendary witches' dance, became wilder and wilder, the figures rose faster and faster. Then suddenly the cock crowed, the night was over, and the witch, exhausted and disillusioned, found herself back in her old kitchen. The cock in this case was Dr. Hjalmar Schacht, President of the *Reichsbank*, who with his enormous stand-up collar did indeed rather resemble a rooster.

Literature is an international undertaking, and I personally had little to complain of during the Inflation. My family of eight was able to live tolerably well on the $25 I received each month from the American literary magazine *The Dial* for a letter from Germany. One of my sons was at a boarding school in the country. Every term I gave him $5 for his fees, which the headmaster received with satisfaction and gratitude. Other pupils brought silver plates, editions of the classics, live geese, or nothing at all. It was best to have one's children in the country at that time, for life in the cities was mad.

My youngest daughter sat on her rocking-horse and called out: 'The Dollar is up!' when the horse's head rose. The same words were sung to the first notes of Beethoven's Fifth Symphony, which have now become a symbol of victory. People spoke of nothing but marks, dollars, and pounds, and the streets of the big cities resembled nothing so much as a stock exchange gone wild. The bars and night-clubs were full to bursting with profiteers spending their ill-gotten gains by the handful.

A severe inflation is the worst kind of revolution. The stern measures – currency restrictions, curtailed production, draconic taxes – that a government can and sometimes must take systematically are nothing by comparison. For there is neither system nor justice in the expropriation and redistribution of property resulting from inflation. A cynical 'each man for himself' becomes the rule of life. But only the most powerful, the most resourceful and unscrupulous, the hyenas of economic life, can come through unscathed. The great mass of those who put their trust in the traditional order, the innocent and unworldly, all those who do productive and useful work, but don't know how to manipulate money, the elderly who hoped to live on what they earned in the past – all these are doomed to suffer. An experience of this kind poisons the morale of a nation.

A straight line runs from the madness of the German Inflation to the madness of the Third Reich. Just as the Germans saw their marks inflated into millions and billions and in the end bursting, so they were later to see their state inflated into 'the *Reich* of all the Germans', 'the German Living Space' 'the New Europe', and 'the New World Order', and so too they will see it burst. In those days the market woman who without batting an eyelash demanded a hundred million for an egg, lost the capacity for surprise. And nothing that has happened since has been insane or cruel enough to surprise her.

It was during the inflation that the Germans forgot how to rely on themselves as individuals and learned to expect everything from 'politics', from the 'state', from 'destiny'. They learned to look on life as a wild adventure, the outcome of which depended not on their own effort but on sinister, mysterious forces. The millions who were then robbed of their wages and savings became the 'masses' with whom Dr. Goebbels was to operate.

Inflation is a tragedy that makes a whole people cynical, hardhearted and indifferent. Having been robbed, the Germans became a nation of robbers.

INFLATION

Walt Rostow

HOW WE CAN CURE IT

Walt Rostow is Professor of Economics at the University of Texas.

The first thing you should know about a speaker is his bias. This is particularly important if he is talking about an issue of public policy, like inflation. I do, indeed, bring to this subject a personal bias. I do not like inflation. Its effects are unfair. The least advantaged groups in society generally suffer the most. Moreover, inflation distorts the pattern of economic and social progress, and erodes the provisions we make for our families' future security.

I also bring to the subject a professional bias. My perspective is that of an economist and historian. I have spent a good deal of my life studying how the world economy has evolved since the end of the 18th century. Now, after some 40 years at the job, I am setting down what I think I have learned. I am trying to put between covers the story of the world economy over the past two centuries, and to do so in ways which help illuminate the large economic issues we confront as a human race: the rate of population increase in the southern half of the world; the problems of food, energy supply and the environment; the reorganisation of our trade and monetary systems and the flow of assistance to the less advantaged developing regions. Among the issues on our common agenda is, evidently, the problem of controlling inflation. What I have to say here is a kind of interim report on how our present inflationary disarray looks from the perspective of an economist-historian.

In fact, it looks very queer indeed. To understand how queer, it is useful to go back three centuries. I have before me a chart showing the British cost of living from 1661 to 1974. It is in the form of an index in which 1913 equals 100. At the time of the Restoration, the cost of living was slightly above 100. Over the next century, it fluctuates well below that level – round about 75. Fluctuations mainly depended on the luck of the harvests and the times of war and peace. From about 1760 to 1793, it rises gently back to 100, as the population increased and Britain began to become dependent on food imports.

The inflation during the French Revolutionary and Napoleonic Wars lifted the consumer price index to almost 200 in the worst year. But after 1815, peace brought a great decline – at first rapid, then slow. By mid-century, the index is down as low as 85. Prices fell because industrial progress was making it cheaper to produce and to transport what was produced.

Then, for a time, industrial progress was offset by other forces. Those forces raised prices sharply from 1852 to 1854, and kept them between 100 and 120 until 1873. The Crimean and other wars contributed to this mildly inflationary period, as did gold-mining in California and Australia, and the time it took to open up the grain fields of the Middle West. The potato had reached its limit in Ireland and elsewhere in Europe as populations increased and the cities grew. The agricultural resources of the New World were called in to redress the balance of the Old.

After 1873, there is another price decline. For a quarter of a century, there are virtually no wars; the American grain pours in, along new railway lines and in increasingly efficient ships; while the march of technology keeps cutting costs in manufacture. By 1895, the price index is down to 70.

Once again, there is a reversal and a rise to 100 in the base year, 1913. The same three factors are at work that produced the high range of prices until 1873: wars – in South Africa and elsewhere; gold-mining; and the cost of opening up some new territories. These were needed because the capacity of the United States to export wheat fell away with the end of the frontier, the increase in America's population, and the growth of its industrial cities. This time, Canada, Argentina, Australia and the Ukraine fulfilled the role of the American West half a century earlier. On the eve of the First World War, then, the British consumer price index was at just about the same level as it had been two and a half centuries earlier, when Charles II came to the throne.

The First World War produced another period of inflation which continued until 1920. The index was then 250. But, once again, there is a decline, Europe did not fully recover before the Great Depression of the 1930s struck; and until the late 1930s, there was a world surplus of foodstuffs and raw materials. In 1933, our index was about 140; and it had risen to only 160 in 1939, despite the demands of rearmament.

During the Second World War, price controls were quite effective in Britain. The price index rose much less than it did during the First World War: to a level around 200. The Korean

War brought it as high as 255 – about the same level as 1920.

Now comes the queer part of the story. Instead of declining after the Korean War, the index continued to move up; and it did so despite a generation of relatively cheap foodstuffs and raw materials. By 1960, the index is almost 350; by 1970, it has crossed 500; in 1974, it averaged 760; by 18 February 1975, it had reached 854. In the spring of 1975, British inflation was moving ahead at an annual rate of more than 40 per cent.

The British economy was evidently out of hand, like a dog chasing his tail. Obviously, the government will have to act, and, for what it is worth, I would recommend a solution I have long regarded as the best. It was proposed in the 1930s by E.F.M. Durbin, and analysed sympathetically by John Maynard Keynes in his *General Theory*. The solution is a protracted wage freeze, accompanied by strong, credible measures to ensure that increases in productivity are passed on to the consumer in lower prices. Fixed money wages and falling prices is the right formula not only for Britain, but also for the rest of Western Europe, Japan and the United States. I say this because we are dealing not with a purely British problem, but with an epidemic.

The story of inflation after the Second World War is not uniform among the major industrial nations of the democratic world. Some, like Germany, have done better, some worse. But the differences, while significant, are relatively minor. We have all experienced protracted and accelerated inflation never before known in times of peace. For a historian, therefore, the questons are: why has this unprecedented rate of inflation occurred; and why has the rate of inflation progressively increased?

Historically, as we have seen, there were two types of inflation: demand-pull inflation and raw-materials-push inflation. The first was the product of a strong demand, the latter was the product of a relative shortage of supply. Periods of strong demand occurred not only during wars, but also towards the peak of trade cycles in times of peace; for example, in 1818, 1825 and 1845. Periods of prosperity leave a greater mark on price indexes when they are accompanied by shortages of food or raw materials. This was the case during the cotton shortage of 1833-35, the food shortage of 1852-54, the coal shortages of 1871-73 and at the end of the century. The more intense inflationary periods brought with them pressures to increase wages. If one looks at wage rates over long periods of history, they tended to remain remarkably stable, except for times of severe inflation. A wage-rate chart looks like an irregular stairway, with steps occurring during times of inflation. Such wage increases generally failed fully to compensate the worker for increases in the cost of living. In peaceful times of rapidly increasing productivity, when prices were falling, wages stayed steady. Therefore, the real income of labour tended to rise most in such periods. Falling prices have been the working man's friend.

Turning to the period after the Second World War, there are two phases when high food and raw material prices played an important part in inflation: from 1945 to 1951, when agricultural and raw material production lagged behind the postwar revival of industry; then again from the end of 1972 to about the middle of 1974, when there was, as we all know, a great convulsion in prices of food, of energy and of raw materials. Between 1951 and 1972, however, we have to look elsewhere for the cause of inflation. The prices of food and raw materials relatively declined, easing inflationary pressures within the major industrial economies.

Now, what about demand-pull inflation? Here we confront what might be called the good side of the inflation story. Since the Second World War, the industrialized world has enjoyed lower levels of unemployment and higher rates of growth than any known in the past. The old-fashioned trade cycle did not wholly disappear. It took the form of stop-and-go; that is, of cycles in rates of growth. But the stop phases of stop-and-go did not result in large increases in unemployment. Business firms expected expansion to resume and they husbanded their labour supply. In effect, we lived for almost 30 years in an economic environment which, in the past, we only knew at peak times of cyclical prosperity.

But this great achievement of social science and public policy introduced a third form of inflation: that is, wage-push inflation. Since the Second World War, wages have risen faster than the average increase in productivity. That kind of wage increase is the basic underlying cause of the chronic inflation of the past 30 years. And once accepted, it tended to accelerate. Under full employment conditions, virtually every organized group in the economy has great bargaining leverage. The unions began to ask more and more in wage settlements: in part, they did this to compensate for past and expected future inflation; in part, they did it to redress what they believed were old inequities. Without accepted new rules of the game, and without the old discipline of cyclical unemployment, our societies passively acquiesced. That is why inflation got out of hand; and that is why a wage freeze is the heart of the remedy.

The dilemma we face is, therefore, clear enough: how can democratic societies achieve the inner discipline and consensus necessary to control wages, without sacrificing the advantages of low levels of unemployment and high rates of growth? On the basis of the experience of the past 30 years, it is easy to be pessimistic. Most advanced industrial nations have tried one formula or another. There have been periods of relative success. But no democratic society has, for long, been able to sustain policies of wage-price discipline.

Nevertheless, looking ahead, I am a temperate optimist in this matter, for two reasons. First, it is palpably true that what we have been doing in recent years endangers the whole fabric of our societies as well as our security.

Second, it is in the interest of labour and business to stop inflation. I have known many labour leaders in many countries. Not one would deny in private that labour, on balance, suffers from inflation. Businessmen, in the short run, can believe they command the power over prices to protect themselves from inflation. But I know of no serious businessman who does not understand that, over a period of time, inflation is also against his interests. This is so because inflation causes stop-and-go policies: and profits are volatile. Inflation is the enemy of profits as well as of the worker's real wage.

If this is the case – if labour and business both have an interest in stopping inflation – why has it proved so difficult? The answer lies in the difficulty of satisfying three conditions. First, in any successful incomes policy or social contract, the various labour leaders must feel confident that they will not lose *vis-à-vis* one another. Labour leaders live in a highly competitive world. They must be able to prove to their constituencies that some other group did not do better than they did. This problem is acute because wage contracts are negotiated at different times. A wage freeze, for example, is likely to prove advantageous to a union which recently negotiated a new contract, less advantageous to a union which negotiated its last contract a year or so earlier. This problem can only be solved by installing an incomes policy for a long period (say, five years), and permitting an initial phase of relative wage adjustment.

Second, the labour leaders, as a group, must feel confident that their self-discipline will not be exploited by business to generate excessive profits. This requires careful monitoring of productivity, profits and prices by the government, including, if necessary, special excess-profit taxes.

Third, and ultimately most important, the vast majority of the citizens, including labour union members and their wives, must perceive that the ending of inflation is in their interest as well as that of the national community. Only then can labour leaders command the support of the rank and file; only then can those who see in inflation a device for overturning democratic societies be frustrated. But if those three conditions can be satisfied, I believe wage-price policies can be carried out and sustained indefinitely in democratic societies.

But, behind them, lies a still more basic question: our sense of direction as nations and as a civilisation. The ultimate question posed by the issue of inflation is whether we, in the advanced industrial part of the democratic world, can recapture a sense of purpose and a will to shape our common destiny. We certainly ought to, for great challenges lie before us. Cheap energy is gone for a long time. We shall have to create new sources of energy for the future; keep the air and water clean; economize in the use of raw materials and develop new ones. We shall have to face the problems of food and population on a world basis. We shall have to work out new relationships between the early and late-comers to industrialization if we are to avoid a neo-mercantilist struggle in which we squabble meanly for scarce resources at great cost to all the parties concerned.

But the political life of our nations has not yet been geared to this new agenda. In a sense, we were a little spoiled by the ease with which we were able to manage the great 30-years boom after the Second World War. It did not prove much of a trick to maintain relatively full employment, and for Western Europe and Japan to become, essentially, as rich as America. Now we are up to more serious business. It requires that we think as national communities and as a world community. And, so far, we have not made much of a job of it. I suspect that only when we realize that we shall have to struggle and work together to preserve and enhance what we have inherited, and reach out in new ways to the nations and peoples who wish to become as affluent as we are, that we will also be able to cure ourselves of democracy's most dangerous disease – inflation.

FUTURE PROSPECTS

Michael Jefferson

FUTURE PROSPECTS

The greatest tyranny has the smallest beginnings. From precedents overlooked, from remonstrances despised, from grievances treated with ridicule, from powerless men oppressed with impunity, and overbearing men tolerated with complacence, springs the tyrannical usage which generations of wise and good men may hereafter perceive and lament and resist in vain. At present, common minds no more see a crushing tyranny in a trivial unfairness or a ludicrous indignity, than the eye uninformed by reason can discern the oak in the acorn, or the utter desolation of winter in the first autumnal fall. Hence the necessity of denouncing with unwearied and even troublesome perseverance a single act of oppression. Let it alone and it stands on record. The country has allowed it and when it is at last provoked to a late indignation it finds itself gagged with the record of its own ill compulsion.

The Times
August 11, 1846

Several of the main industrial nations had, temporarily at least, managed to get inflation fairly well under control by late 1976 aided by the effects of sluggish business activity and a good harvest. Of those major nations which still did not have inflation under control – their number also included Italy, France and Belgium – the United Kingdom economy was boxed in by the errors of past policies to a spectacular degree. Because of the severity of its problems as well as its particular interest to most of those reading this book, this final chapter concentrates on Britain. There are some lessons here for other countries on what policies *not* to pursue.

How We Got Here

As the year 1976 drew towards its close, the United Kingdom economy was in a parlous state and there were widespread hopes that a large loan from the International Monetary Fund would prevent a descent into the abyss. The fact that, even in such dire circumstances, attitudes and policies had changed so little, and so many counted upon the gambler's last throw, was a measure of complacency and wishful thinking which will prevent any fundamental changes for the better.

The British people have, to an even greater degree than people in other Western nations, lost any positive sense of achievement and progress. The first has been decimated by the politics and economics of envy, and the self-inflicted wounds of social conflict. The second has disappeared as those with the greatest vision have felt embattled by a hostile environment, and have semi-retired in disillusionment. More recently the ravages of inflation have quickened the deterioration in both respects. No better illustration of cause and effect can be found than in the evolution of Britain's middle classes since 1945.

Not always originating in the middle classes, indeed upward social mobility in Britain since the early nineteenth century until recent years has been very marked, the people who composed that group after 1945 were relatively well-educated, often guilt-ridden and uncertain about their role in society, but combining an individualism which hampered a united front with a social awareness which encouraged compromise. They had the knowledge and the sensitivity to understand that the fruits of further economic growth would in large part have to go to those poorer than themselves, and that substantial institutional changes would be required in order that merit might the more easily be recognized and privilege undermined. They had the intelligence to realize that society must work as one, with give and take by all sections of the community, and did not realize until it was much too late that they had done almost all the giving. Income and wealth redistribution was emphasized rather than income and wealth creation, to the point where public policies and attitudes became destructive of both. There could be no better illustration of Edmund Burke's dictum that the people never give up their liberties but under some delusion.

What the middle classes failed to realize was that the politics of envy, inevitably to be succeeded by resentment on all sides, meant taking away not only from the exceedingly rich, but from the rather poor. It meant increasingly, as general economic growth slowed down, that aspirations and expectations were destroyed by the harsh facts of squeezed gross incomes, high marginal tax rates, other income deductions, and the plunderings of nationalised industries and local government offices operating with dubious efficiency. It meant that the politics of envy spread into every facet of life.

The encroachments of bureaucracy and taxation were the spearhead of the attack on achievement and enterprise. The main responses were as negative as the challenges. For some, entry into a cash or barter economy was increasingly resorted to in order to avoid the full rigours of penal taxation. But this required self-employment, whereas for the majority of people who were employed there was no such recourse. Those involved in income and wealth creation had their vigour and confidence sapped, began to think more about leisure than about work, might even drift into the non-marketed sector of the economy. The non-marketed sector of the economy, principally central and local government and public sector agencies, had become a vast employment sink. Worse, it had become a complex bureaucratic network living to a large extent parasitically on the mainly private, marketed sector of the economy.

By 1976, public sector employment in the United Kingdom had topped the five million mark, if we exclude more than two million employees of the nationalized industries and those employed in the Armed Forces, and represented over 22 per cent of total employment. Over the space of fifteen years these public employees had grown from 14 to 22 per cent of those employed, a powerful political force which represented almost the entire growth of employment in the service sector. This growth of service or tertiary sector employment was supposed to be a mark of the advanced and prosperous society, enjoying increased leisure indoors and out, spending large sums on these activities as well as on better health and educational facilities. Instead, this dream had been transformed into an army of paper pushers during a period when teachers came to represent less than half of those employed in education (clerks retaining their jobs while tens of thousands of newly qualified teachers could not find employment) and the number of clerks per bed occupied in the National Health Service almost doubled.

These were just some of the features of a society generating higher and higher inflation. In the pursuit of (over –) full employment public expenditure and employment were maximized, tax revenue rose even when relief would have assisted faster growth and encouraged confidence, and anyone who openly stood against this tide of profligacy was ridiculed. In the end, as the critics had warned, the policies had become self-defeating.

These policies, whether directly aimed against the middle classes or bleeding them progressively whiter by accident, did not bring a sharp and united reaction. Instead, the middle classes seemed to suffer a loss of backbone and gave little evidence of any capacity to stand up and be counted in an effective way. They did not seem to understand that – however undignified – a world of pressure group politics abhors a vacuum which, if the middle classes do not fill it, will be filled by others unsympathetic to their wishes.

Businessmen, largely drawn from the middle classes, were often equally to blame. Few thought they should try to influence events, few recognized that if they did not represent themselves in a vigorous way no-one else would (I leave on one side the mostly rather effete institutions which claimed to do this job and often espoused policies which increased government intervention and public expenditure). Most felt they should work silently within the policies of the country which, given the way the country was moving, was tantamount to mass suicide.

What the middle classes also failed to perceive were the internal contradictions of the movement against which they retreated, and with which they felt some sympathy. These internal contradictions would inevitably destroy the middle classes in any conventional sense within a democratic system, and probably destroy the democratic system itself.

Thus notions of equality of opportunity blending with egalitarianism inevitably ousted the rise of the meritocracy which, during the 1950's and early 1960's, many social commentators believed had occurred and would be reinforced. Policies and institutions which were used to further the interests of newly vocal groups would prove selfdefeating, as both took on a momentum of their own. Policies became more extended in scope, involving general rules, growing inefficiency, and a declining sensitivity to the interest they were originally intended to serve, and thus became less well understood, less coherent and less beneficial. Largely because the collective and universal provision of services was demanded rather than their market and selective provision, institutions became bigger, more remote and less well comprehended. While it was not surprising, if one had any sense of history, that groups given a voice would largely destroy the framework of institutions and communications networks which had given them that voice, the consequences were not widely foreseen. Those wise people who had the necessary foresight to recognize the road to serfdom were, and still are to a considerable degree, dismissed as hopelessly old-fashioned extremists.

There were a number of ideas underlying the drift towards the morass. Some were desirable in theory, but difficult to put into practice. Others, such as some of the worst aspects of neo-Keynesian policies, labour restrictive practices such as the terrifying 'closed shop', fiscal measures designed to achieve social revolution, and the general belief that the government should do something about almost everything, were thoroughly pernicious. They led to the discouragement of savings and investment, high inflation combined with high unemployment, low growth and sluggish consumption, static or declining living standards, and deepening social tensions. This was where the politics of envy had brought the United Kingdom by the end of 1976, and even threatened to disunite its main component parts. It was hardly surprising that morale seemed unable to sink lower, for the policies of successive governments and the continued baying of some politicians could only be construed as intended to eliminate confidence. There was hardly an intelligent, well-educated and gifted person who had not considered emigration and the number acting upon such thoughts was steadily rising.

How We Get Out

Looking to the future, how can Britain recover its confidence and get out of the morass? In a book on inflation it may seem that we have already strayed far beyond the bounds of our subject. Yet, as I tried to show in summarising inflation over the past two thousand years, inflation is both a symptom and a cause of much wider societal issues. A symptom of a wider social malaise, whether of conflict or incompetence; a cause of misery, the destruction of assets and aspirations, and further conflict.

The only way out (and here as elsewhere I am merely stating my personal views) is to step back firmly, in order the better to progress thereafter. Whatever one's view on the desirability of public expenditure, and many believe a high level of public expenditure is the hallmark of a civilised society although it could hardly be called a necessary condition, there can be no doubt that public expenditure has risen far more rapidly than a slowly growing national economy could afford. A 20 per cent real increase in public expenditure over a period when the national economy grew only 2 per cent, as has happened in the mid-1970's, is a recipe for disaster. There is much to be said for cuts in public expenditure, planned over a period of up to ten years to minimise hardship, with the objective of reducing their component in GNP to about one-third of the total from its present level of 53 per cent.

These public expenditure cuts should be real. They must not be achieved by maintaining public sector activities and changing the method of financing, so that the consumer pays for what he or she earlier received as of right and funded through taxation. Private provision of a number of goods and services previously collectively provided would be required, and consumers would pay for these. The cuts should also be selective.

It is often claimed that public expenditure cuts would involve a massive reduction in the quality of health, welfare, other social, and educational services. To anyone who has observed the standards in these services in recent years and knows the structure of employment in them, this is an absurd notion. Since the mid-1960's part-time female employment in local government has increased by over 75 per cent, and full-time female employment has increased by over 40 per cent. The overwhelming bulk of this employment is not at the 'sharp' end of the provision of the main services, much of it performs routine and often unnecessary clerical tasks, and a major cut-back would have minimal adverse consequences on the quality of service provided. It should be added, perhaps, that in an era of high unemployment which may last for some years, it is surely better to declare redundant those who provide a second household income than to deprive households of their sole source of income. Moreover, many medical, social and educational practitioners would welcome the lifting of this bureaucratic burden off their backs. In central government also, many civil servants would not be sorry to see the number of clerks and other low productivity workers cut down.

The importance of these measures is psychological as much as economic, the need to lift some of the burden of bureaucracy, nonproductive activities, and taxation from the wilting shoulders of even those taxpayers earning below average incomes. Indeed, in the short-term public expenditure and employment cuts have some adverse economic consequences. But given the central responsibility of out-of-control public expenditure and employment for the depth of the United Kingdom's present economic plight, this is where the action should be taken steadily over several years. The objective should be to reduce public sector employment, central and local civilian government combined, to no more than three million (about 60% of its present total). It would be totally unacceptable to throw any additional burdens on the long suffering taxpayer.

The second body of measures revolves around the need to bring down taxation rates, to encourage savings and investment, and to revive morale. Taxation rates on earnings which exceed 50% are clearly penal, and their reduction to a maximum 50% from the present rate of 83% would cost little more than £300 mn. in lost revenue annually. This would have the effect of bringing more people more fully back into the tax net: the self-employed would accept the full rigours of taxation more readily if the rates ceased to be penal; those who once did regular freelance work in their spare time, but gave it up because of the high taxation rate and the enormous burdens of dealing with the bureaucracy of the Inland Revenue authorities, might start again; and so on.

The Labour Government's Chancellor of the Exchequer announced various public expenditure cuts and taxation increases on 15th December, 1976. They offered the opportunity to judge whether the long-term objectives of sustained cuts in real public expenditure, public sector employment, and the burden of taxation were likely under present conditions and policies. Despite the furore surrounding the introduction of the measures, they provided little optimism for the future.

Superficially, the most encouraging element in the Chancellor's package was the intention to cut public expenditure in 1977-78 by £1 bn. and in 1978-79 by £1.5 bn. (at 1976 survey prices). In fact this represented a cut-back in public expenditure, supposing it takes place, of less than 4% after a 20% rise in three years of virtual stagnation in the national economy. Moreover, much of the package involved either the imposition of further burdens on the private sector rather than a real reduction of the public sector's claims on resources; or the sorts of measures which may mean postponement of public expenditure rather than real cuts, and even then are liable to have a greater impact on the private sector (such as cuts in housing and other construction). Time and time again over the past fifteen years announced public expenditure cuts have not in the event taken place, as this expenditure appears to have built up a momentum of its own. On taxation, too, there was reference to possible tax cuts in the next Budget and encouragement to those involved in exports, but nothing of substance occurred. Meanwhile the public sector deficit is expected to continue at unacceptably high levels for some years to come.

The touchstone of the measures was the cuts which would have the most direct impact on the least productive of public sector employees. Given the widening concern with the number of paper-pushers in the public sector, and their massive growth in recent years which has led to adverse criticism in places long renowned for blanket support of increased public expenditure, this seemed a good moment to begin a process which could be continued and extended as the economy recovered. In the event, the Chancellor's measures were negligible in this area. Civil Service economies amounting to £30 mn. in 1977-78 and £10 mn in 1978-79 are very small beer, while the Chancellor did no more regarding local government employment than refer to the reduction in the Rate Support Grant from $65\frac{1}{2}$% to 61% in 1977-78 (for England and Wales, with a corresponding reduction for Scotland).

The *Financial Times* had argued in the weeks before the Budget against a huge immediate cut in the public sector borrowing requirement but for cuts which were genuine, ongoing, and wherever possible in current rather than capital spending. On the morrow of the mini-budget their leader article commented: 'Yesterday's package does not measure up to these requirements. It is the very least that the IMF would accept as a condition for allowing the Government the first instalment of the loan for which it has asked'. As far as dealing with Britain's fundamental economic problems was concerned, *The Economist* concluded that the 'measures have not helped by an iota'. These views were self-evidently correct.

The most difficult challenge facing Britain of all, however, is the need for a fundamental shift in attitudes away from the divisive stances adopted in recent years by left-wing politicians. We have wanted societal evolution; they have spoken the language of societal revolution, with disastrous consequences. They have used words like the guillotine and policies like the garotte, chopping others down with shrill rhetoric and letting them die slowly by strangulation from heavier and heavier taxation.

There must be an end to the drift to non-democratic socialism, and instead the restoration of a desire for achievement with its due rewards. A sense of progress must once more be instilled into the population, which can only do 'their own thing' with the minimum of legal regulation and tax disincentives. Finally, there must be an end to wishful thinking and acceptance that unfashionable prescriptions may be required. We must face up to the challenges of our times; speak up and be counted for the restoration of an achieving and income-creating society based upon merit, not privilege; oppose those who would increase the burdens of bureaucracy, large systems and punitive income redistribution.

But such a fundamental shift in attitudes can only occur when our political rulers have a clear vision, the ruled a clear understanding of what has gone wrong and a general determination to put it right by means commonly agreed. The United Kingdom seems some years off that point still, but from 1978 the increasing impact of North Sea oil may give politicians more room for manoeuvre, policy-makers greater scope for doing good, and the British people grounds for more optimism. Much will depend on how wise public policy is: will it maximise the long-term benefits to the British economy, and to our society at large; or will this seedcorn be frittered away in the same prodigal spirit which has marred so much post-war policy?

Before moving on to the prospects for inflation, however, it must be recognised that the relatively simple remedies suggested here in terms of public expenditure cuts and the encouragement of savings and investment may prove to be too simplistic. Nevertheless, I believe that without these steps at least some of the necessary preconditions for greater economic prosperity will not have been met.

The Prospects for Inflation

Any view of the prospects for inflation, therefore, which does not take political, social and economic forces more generally into account is doomed to failure. And because there can be no single view of the outcome of the enormous challenges facing the British economy, its political system and its social fabric, there can be no single view of how inflation will proceed.

The prospects can be analysed under four headings:

(i) Continued drift, whereby the democratic system continues to serve solely as an arena for increasingly debilitating conflict, where the dictatorship of the majority as manipulated by politicians of the Left holds sway, where wishful thinking and a refusal to take firm action to stop the rot persists, and where inflationary pressure continues to be insurmountable. This view implies frequent periods of double-digit inflation, but is not a long-term state of equilibrium as the societal pressures are not sustainable and collapse occurs.

(ii) Provided collective action is not so long delayed as to make the situation wholly irretrievable, mounting societal pressures operating within the democratic system and reinforced by the mass media cause a halt to inflationary policies. Corrective action is taken on excessive past expenditures in the public sector, continued pressure is exerted on public sector spending to undermine inflationary pressures from this source, new emphasis is placed on income creation, action is taken against monopolistic and other restrictive practices by labour as well as capital, and the money supply is constrained to avoid being itself a cause of instability. This is the 'liberal dream', but it would get inflation under permanent control.

(iii) The situation continues to deteriorate, declining groups become the seedbed of fascism, and democracy is overthrown in favour of authoritarian rule from the notional political Right. Inflation may be brought successfully under control; if not, steps will almost certainly be taken to safeguard the position of the middle-class and artisans' groups responsible for the rise of authoritarianism. Although the rise of fascism in the past has been caused by more than economic crisis provoked by the idiocies of left-wing politicians, in particular the existence of attitudes which certain social classes held which prepared them to interpret their economic experience in ways favourable to rising fascist groups, there must now be concern that official policies are severely undermining the traditional tolerance and sounder reasoning in British society.

(iv) The situation continues to deteriorate, but no successful backlash occurs, and finally a small minority from the extreme left succeeds to power and wields it no less ruthlessly than in the preceding case. Inflation is apparently brought under control because the normal price mechanism is abolished, but chronic shortages and black markets indicate the underlying realities. This is the result which many Marxists and Trotskyites currently seek, although few of them are likely to survive and prosper in the conditions they have created.

These are the four main prospects for inflation. The situation has long since gone beyond the point where palliatives could be successful, supposing they ever have been in more normal conditions. Thus the reader will look in vain for laudatory references to incomes policies, social contracts and the like. These may be part of a psychological war to induce a greater sense of responsibility among the major constituents of our society. Of themselves they are, in the great battle against inflation, a mere will o' the wisp. At the present juncture Britain is headed on course (i), which is likely to make either course (iii) or (iv) unavoidable. However, a growing number of voices have been heard in recent months which may indicate a shift to course (ii) is still possible. Unfortunately, commentators on the British scene in recent years have all too often been over-optimistic, and at times like the present it is not wishful thinking which will generate the preconditions for desirable change.

INDEX